AdWords Workbook:

Advertising on Google AdWords, YouTube, & The Display Network

2018 Edition

by Jason McDonald, Ph.D.

© 2018, JM Internet Group

https://www.jm-seo.org/

Tel. 800-298-4065

THE "NEW" ADWORDS INTERFACE

Google has rolled out a **new interface** to AdWords, which remains in "beta" at the time of this writing. Accordingly, I have done my best throughout this book to give you step-by-step instructions and screenshots from the new interface. I recommend using the new interface.

Here's how to can *switch* between the "old" and the "new."

> To switch to the "**new**" interface from the "old" interface, simply click on the "gear" icon on the top right and then select "Try the faster AdWords."

> To switch back to the "**old**" interface from the "new" interface, simply click on the "wrench" icon on the top right, and then select "Return to previous AdWords."

Watch a **video** from Google on the New AdWords Experience at **http://jmlinks.com/39q** and access the help file at **http://jmlinks.com/39r**. Be sure to register your Workbook, as I will periodically post updates to the book's registration page as Google is still adjusting the new interface, and thus some of the screenshots and instructions in this Workbook may become out-of-date. That's Google for you!

If you have questions, please email me at **j.mcdonald@jm-seo.net** or send a question via **http://jmlinks.com/contact**. You can also call **AdWords tech support** at 866-246-6453 or 844-756-8495 (hidden at the top right under the "?" icon in the new interface, or under the "gear" icon in the old interface) and ask for help switching from one interface to the other.

CONTENTS

0
INTRODUCTION

Welcome to the *AdWords Workbook, 2018 edition*! This book teaches you how to advertise your business via Google's proprietary ad system, *AdWords*.

AdWords is how to advertise on Google.

*The book explains - in plain English - how to use AdWords **effectively**.*

AdWords is **powerful**! AdWords is **complicated**! AdWords is **expensive**! AdWords is **fun**!

Three quarters of the above statements are true, and AdWords can be your best friend or your worst enemy. Indeed, many people don't realize that AdWords isn't just a way to advertise your product or service on the *Google search engine*. It's also a way to get your company, product, or service on Google's network of affiliated sites called the *Display Network* that includes blogs, parked domains, portals, newspapers and even YouTube and Gmail. And it's a method of *remarketing*, "tagging" your website visitors so you can show and reshow them your ad until they're ready to buy. It's even a method to advertise on apps on mobile phones.

This workbook will teach you the *lies* and *secrets*, *tips* and *tricks*, *tactics* and *techniques* that will help you leverage **AdWords** to get your company, product or service to the top of Google, in video ads on YouTube, into email ads on Gmail, and placed on a cornucopia of websites in the Google Display Network (GDN) as both images and text. It will also show you the power of *remarketing*, how to get your ads in front of potential customers by following them across the Internet. The goal is to first understand how best to use AdWords, and then to set up AdWords advertising in the most efficient way possible, spending the *least* while getting the *most* from each advertising dollar.

A Love / Hate Relationship

I am a lover of AdWords, and I am a powerful critic of AdWords. I love AdWords, and I hate AdWords!

AdWords, you see, is like alcohol. Used wisely and with restraint, it can be quite fun and quite productive. Used poorly and with reckless abandon, it can burn through your budget and drive you to bankruptcy (and more alcohol).

ADWORDS IS LIKE ALCOHOL

I am not alone (*especially on the love part*). There are many books on AdWords, and there are literally thousands of AdWords advertising companies and consultants who have all drunk the *Google Kool-Aid* and will all spout the *Google Gospel* on AdWords. In Google's own words:

> *Be seen by customers at the very moment that they're searching on Google for the things you offer. And only pay when they click to visit your website or call.* (***https://adwords.google.com/home***).

Sounds incredible, no? Be seen on the world's most prolific search engine at the moment of search, and only pay when they click.

Yes, AdWords *is* effective. AdWords *is* incredible.

The Dark Side of AdWords

But there's a dark side to AdWords that few people know about, and even fewer talk about, publicly. I am relatively alone in "going public" to educate the general public, especially small business owners and marketers, about the dark side of AdWords – the ways in which AdWords is full of traps, or what I call *gotchas,* that can literally waste thousands of your hard-earned dollars.

There is a bit of a conspiracy of silence around AdWords...but

Friends don't let friends drive drunk, and *friends don't let friends use AdWords without understanding its pitfalls and problems.*

An Advertiser Walks into a Bar

Imagine you go into a bar, looking for a nice beverage to slake your thirst. You ask the bartender, "Hey, Bartender! Get me a Whiskey!" Now, perhaps you want the *cheapest* whiskey, or perhaps you want to spend no more than $19.00 a glass (you have a taste for *Glenmorangie Milsean* whiskey). But, if you do not specify the whiskey, the bartender is incentivized to give you his most *profitable* whiskey, is he not?

GOOGLE IS LIKE A BARTENDER

Indeed, if you think about the business relationship between the bartender and you the patron in the cold, sober light of day, you'll realize that the bartender is incentivized to "get you drunk," to "run up a big tab," and he'll happily serve you his most profitable and expensive whiskey all night long. Then, if you get in your car, and crash against a tree, he may say, "it's not his fault." Even worse, an unscrupulous bartender might "water down the whiskey" and serve you an inferior product yet charge you the full price.

The Bartender is incentivized to sell you the most expensive, profitable whiskey.

You, in contrast, may want the cheapest whiskey, or at least to make a pro-active choice as to what you want to drink on the continuum from cheap to expensive when it comes to whiskeys. Or maybe you don't drink, and you want an apple juice or diet Coke. That's OK, too.

And

The Bartender is "not responsible" if you drink too much and wreck your car.

You, however, would rather not wreck your car.

Google, you see, is like the bartender, and you are like the patron. Google gets paid by the *click*, whereas you get paid by the *conversion* (a *sale* on your e-Commerce site or a *sales lead* such as a completed feedback form on your website).

Those are not necessarily the same thing, my friend. (More about this later).

We'll circle back to the contradictions and tensions between you and Google in AdWords in the next Chapter, but for now just keep in mind that Google is a for-profit corporation, not a charity and, understandably, it rigs AdWords to maximize its profits.

Zig from the Negative, Back to the Positive

One of the things you'll learn in AdWords is that it is non-linear. You can't explain it or understand it in a straight line; rather, you have to *zig*, and *zag*, to understand its power and its complexities. So leaving aside the skepticism about Google, AdWords, and any conflicts of interest, let's review five ways that AdWords is a powerful advertising tool:

AdWords can –

1. Get your company, product, or service to the **top of Google** at the precise moment, for the precise keywords that your customers are searching for, just as they're ready to buy a product or service.
2. Get your company, product, or service onto **thousands of websites and blogs** that participate in the **Google Display Network**, allowing you to reach customers as they **browse** the Web for information.
3. **Follow your customers "around the Internet"** through **remarketing**, showing them your ads on Google, YouTube, and thousands upon thousands of independent websites in the Google Display Network.
4. Get your company, product, or service onto **YouTube**, the #1 video site on the Internet, and **Gmail**, the #1 free email service.

5. Market your **App** to interested consumers through in-App advertising.

If you know what you're doing, AdWords can be an incredibly effective tool in your advertising and marketing toolbox.

Enter the AdWords Workbook

To succeed at AdWords without wasting money, you need an expert guide and an expert guidebook. That's what this Workbook is. It will teach you secrets, tips, tricks, and techniques to effectively use Google AdWords to market your product or service in the most efficient manner possible. We will proceed, together, "eyes wide open," understanding that Google is like a bartender or a used car salesman that has good – *no great* – products to offer us as advertisers, even if he's incentivized to oversell us just a tad.

AdWords is powerful, and you and I are going to learn, together, how to unleash its power to help your business in an effective and cost-efficient manner.

Isn't that exciting? I think it is. I love AdWords, and use it for myself and my clients. And I am going to teach you how to use it *safely* and *effectively*.

Who is This Workbook For?

This workbook is aimed primarily at **small business owners** and **marketing managers**. **Non-profits** will also find it useful. If you have a product or service to sell, and you realize that your customers go to Google, to websites such as blogs or news sites, to YouTube, or to Gmail, this workbook will help you understand how to use AdWords efficiently to "get the word out."

If you are a person whose job involves **advertising**, **marketing**, and/or **branding**, this workbook is for you. If you are a small business that sees a marketing opportunity in online advertising of any type, this workbook is for you. And if your job is to market a business or organization online in today's Internet economy, this book is for you. Anyone who wants to look behind the curtain and understand the mechanics of how to use Google AdWords (including the Google Display Network, remarketing, YouTube, and/or Gmail) will benefit from this book.

Anyone who sees – however dimly or skeptically – that online advertising could help their business can (and will) benefit from this workbook.

Here's our **game plan**, Chapter by Chapter:

1. **AdWords Basics** – an overview of the basic logic and structure of AdWords. Pg. 16
2. **AdWords Gotchas** – an emergency checkup of the major gotchas in AdWords, and how to stop them immediately. Pg. 36
3. **Keywords** – how to brainstorm valuable keywords and build an organized Keyword Worksheet. Pg. 58
4. **The Search Network** – how to use AdWords effectively on Google.com and its so-called "Search Partners" like Yelp and Comcast. Pg. 98
5. **The Display Network** – a deep dive into Google's troublesome partner network (officially called AdSense or the Google Display Network (GDN)) Pg. 180
6. **YouTube Advertising** – explore the power of video to market your company, product, or service on Google's YouTube service. Pg. 220
7. **AdWords Metrics**. Using AdWords and Google Analytics to measure your return on investment. Pg. 236
8. **AdWords Toolbook** – a cornucopia of AdWords learning resources, tools, blogs, and other websites to help you master AdWords and keep up-to-date on online advertising. Pg. 272

>> MEET THE AUTHOR

My name is Jason McDonald, and I have been active on the Internet since 1994 (*having invented the Internet along with Al Gore*) and taught SEO, AdWords, and Social Media since 2009 – online, at Stanford University Continuing Studies, at both AcademyX and the Bay Area Video Coalition in San Francisco, at workshops, and in corporate trainings across these United States. I love figuring out how things work, and I love teaching others! AdWords advertising is an endeavor that I understand, and I want to empower you to understand it as well.

I am AdWords Certified and manage thousands of client dollars each month on AdWords as well as on Bing's advertising platform. I also manage ads on YouTube, Facebook, and LinkedIn plus do SEO (Search Engine Optimization) and SMM (Social Media Marketing). This makes me uniquely qualified to be objective about AdWords; AdWords is only one of the tools in our toolkit, and we want to use it when it's the best tool (but not when another tool like SEO, Facebook, or Twitter would be a better choice).

Learn more about me at **https://www.jasonmcdonald.org/** or at my corporate website **https://www.jm-seo.org/**. Or just call 800-298-4065, say something flattering, and my secretary will put you through. *(Like I have a secretary! Just call if you have something to ask or say)*. Visit the websites above to follow me on Twitter, connect with me on LinkedIn, or like me on Facebook. *Sorry, my Snapchat feed is so crazy it's for friends and family, only.*

» SPREAD THE WORD: TAKE A SURVEY & GET $5 OR A FREE BOOK!

If you like this workbook, please take a moment to take a short **survey**. The survey helps me find errors in the book, learn from student questions, and get feedback to improve future editions. Plus, by taking the survey, I'll be able to reach out to you, and we can even become friends. Or, if not friends, at least friends on the Internet or Facebook which isn't quite the same thing, but it's still pretty good!

Here's how –

1. Visit **http://jmlinks.com/survey**.
2. Take a short **survey** about the book.
3. I will rebate you $5 via Amazon gift eCard.

How's that for an offer you can't refuse?

This offer is limited to the first 100 participants, and only for participants who have purchased a paid copy of the book. You may be required to show proof of purchase and the birth certificate of your firstborn child, cat, or goldfish. If you don't have a child, cat, or goldfish, you may be required to prove telepathically that you bought the book.

» QUESTIONS AND MORE INFORMATION

I **encourage** my students to ask questions! If you have questions, submit them via **http://jmlinks.com/contact**. There are two sorts of questions: ones that I know instantly, for which I'll zip you an email answer right away, and ones I do not know instantly, in which case I will investigate, and we'll figure out the answer together.

As a teacher, I learn most from my students. So please don't be shy!

>> COPYRIGHT AND DISCLAIMER

Additional Disclaimer. Internet marketing is an art, and not a science. Any changes to your Internet marketing strategy, including SEO, Social Media Marketing, and AdWords, is at your own risk. Neither Jason McDonald, Excerpti Communications, Inc., nor the JM Internet Group nor my Black Labrador, Buddy, assumes any responsibility for the effect of any changes you may, or may not, make to your website or AdWords advertising based on the information in this workbook.

Additional Additional Disclaimer. Please keep your arms and legs in the vehicle at all times, be kind to one another, and signal while turning left, especially on Thursdays.

▶▶ REGISTER YOUR WORKBOOK FOR ONLINE TOOLS

This workbook is meant to leverage the power of the Internet. **Register** your copy online to get a PDF copy of this book (with clickable links to make it easy to access online resources). You'll also get free access to my *AdWords Dashboard* and *AdWords Toolbook*, which identify my absolute favorite free tools all set out for you to use in easy click-to-go format.

Here's how to **register** your copy of this workbook:

1. Go to **https://jm-seo.org/workbooks**
2. Click on *AdWords Workbook 2018.*
3. Use this password: **adwords18**
4. You're in. Simply click on the link for a PDF copy of the *Workbook* as well as access to the worksheets referenced herein.

Once you register, you get access to –

- **A PDF copy of this book**. Read it on your PC or tablet, and the links referenced in the book become clickable. This is a great way to extend the book into the myriad resources such as example websites or social media pages, FAQ's, support or help from the major vendors, and videos.
- **My AdWords dashboard** – an easy-to-use, clickable list of the best tools for AdWords by category (e.g., keywords tools, ad preview tools, etc.).
- **The *AdWords Toolbook*** – a collection of up-to-date social media tools in detail. While the *Dashboard* identifies my favorites, the *Toolbook* compiles the universe of free AdWords tools.

Jump Codes

Throughout the book, I reference the website JMLINKS.com (**http://jmlinks.com/**) plus various "jump codes." If you're reading in PDF format, the links are clickable. If you're reading in hard copy or on the Kindle, I advise you to fire up your Web browser, bookmark **http://jmlinks.com/** and then enter the codes.

Here's a screenshot:

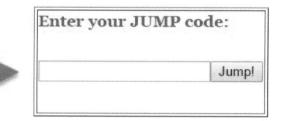

For example, **http://jmlinks.com/16s** would mean first go to **http://jmlinks.com/** and enter "16s" in the jump code box. Your browser will then "jump" you to the referenced resource.

> **VIDEO.** Watch a video tutorial on how to use "jump" codes at **http://jmlinks.com/jump**.

>> ACKNOWLEDGEMENTS

No man is an island. I would like to thank my beloved wife, Noelle Decambra, for allowing me to dive deeply into online marketing, and for being my personal cheerleader in the book industry. Gloria McNabb has done her usual tireless job as first assistant, including updating this edition as well the *AdWords Toolbook*. I would also like to thank my Black Labrador retriever, Buddy, for countless walks and games of fetch, during which I refined my ideas about online advertising and about life. I would also like to thank my students and clients who have given me the trust and privilege to manage their accounts in AdWords. There is nothing quite like learning by doing, and I appreciate that opportunity.

And, again, a huge thank you to my students – online, in San Francisco, and at Stanford Continuing Studies. You challenge me, you inspire me, and you motivate me!

Let's get started!

1

ADWORDS BASICS

If you were lucky enough to plan a vacation to Brazil, you'd probably buy a guidebook to the South American country such as Lonely Planet's *Lonely Planet Brazil* (**http://jmlinks.com/23f**). You might read the book on the plane ride down, and before you planned out your itinerary for what's *fun at Carnival* or a trip to *Encontro das Aguas* (where the Amazon and the Rio Negro rivers combine at **http://jmlinks.com/23w**), you'd want a general overview to the country. Your goal would be to "not get lost" in Brazil (e.g., inside the Amazon jungle), to "not get robbed," and in a positive sense, to make the most out of your investment of time and money for your Brazilian vacation. You'd marvel at the beauty, success, and intrigue of Brazil, but you'd also realize that – like all countries – Brazil has its bad neighborhoods and weird cultural quirks. *AdWords is like Brazil*: enormous, complicated, with a scary jungle, key cities, different regions, wonderful, honest people, and scary thieves, etc. Read this Chapter on "AdWords Basics" "as if" you were on a plane ride from your home city to the country of *AdWordsLandia*.

Let's get started!

TODO LIST:

>> Search vs. Browse

>> Keyword Targeting

>> Bids and the Quality Score Conundrum

>> Why Use AdWords?

>> Elements of Ads on AdWords

>> AdWords Organization

>> Getting Online Help with AdWords

⟫ SEARCH VS. BROWSE

AdWords is not one, but two, very different networks. Like the muddy *Rio Negro* in Brazil and the relatively clear *Amazon* at the *Encontro das Aguas*, it is two rivers – yes they meet and interact, but it is two – not one – products. Google does its best to muddy the waters and confuse businesses into just throwing money at AdWords, but your advertising dollars will be much more effective if you keep in mind that Google AdWords is two distinct and different networks, and if you have a clear head as to "which network" you are targeting at which time.

A good way to understand the two networks is to distinguish between "search" vs. "browse." We'll use as an example *Jason's Cat Emporium* of San Francisco, California, a hypothetical business that offers a) cat boarding, b) cat grooming and c) cat toys. *We don't do dogs, and we certainly don't do iguanas!* It's cats 24/7.

Turning to our target customers, we realize that there are two very different scenarios that are relevant to Google advertising.

Scenario #1 Search. The customer is pro-actively **searching** for "cat boarding." He's leaving San Francisco on a ten-week tour to Brazil, and he wants someone to take care of his prize cat, Kittles. He pro-actively searches on Google, entering in search queries such as *cat boarding San Francisco, quality cat hotels, cat sitters*, etc. This search methodology corresponds to what Google calls the "Search Network," which is Google.com plus sites like Yelp.com or Comcast.net (called "Search Partners") that have a strong search orientation. In some situations, YouTube search also functions in this way (e.g., "How to potty train a kitten" as a search on YouTube).

Scenario #2 Browse. Here, the customer is not pro-actively searching for "cat boarding." Rather, he is reading up on blogs on cat-related issues, such as CatBehaviorAssociates.com (**http://jmlinks.com/23h**) or an article on the ChicagoTribune.com entitled, "The Last Free-ranging Cat library in Illinois" (**http://jmlinks.com/23j**). Note that he is not entering in keywords to search; rather, he is just reading blogs and newspaper sites that may, or may not, be about cats and cat care. This pattern of **browsing**, but not searching, corresponds to what Google calls the Google Display Network ("GDN" or just

"Display Network" for short), which is not Google.com at all but partner sites like CatBehaviorAssociates.com and ChicagoTribune.com that agree to allow Google to place ads on their websites. (He may also be browsing YouTube videos that relate to cats). Indeed, **remarketing** (following users around the Web and showing them relevant ads) is part of this browsing process.

VIDEO. Watch an official video tutorial on the Google Search Network as well as the Google Display Network at **http://jmlinks.com/23g**. **Note**: be aware that it's overly positive and fails to explain the relevant gotchas!

Pro-actively Choose Your Network

You, as an advertiser, should be **pro-active** about which network you want to run ads on, and it really is a function of how strongly you feel people "search" for your products or services or whether you feel that they are more likely to be "browsing" for something similar to your product or service. Note that if someone is pro-actively searching for your product or service they are much more likely to convert, as opposed to if they are just browsing blogs, websites, and YouTube and just "happen" to see an ad for your company.

VIDEO. Watch a video from Google on Campaign Types and Google Networks at **http://jmlinks.com/26d**.

As we shall see in Chapter 2 on "Gotchas," Google defaults you into *both* the Search and the Display Network, but – for most advertisers – the Display Network is much more difficult and has a *much, much, much, much, much, much, much* lower ROI (return on investment). Among the reasons (as we will explain in detail in Chapter 5 on the Google Display Network) is that the GDN has many nefarious or I might argue, even fraudulent, websites that do nothing but generate spurious clicks. An example would be what is called a "Parked Domain" such as Kitty.com (**http://jmlinks.com/23k**). (Note that official Google policy bans ads on Parked Domains (**http://jmlinks.com/23m**), but Google seems to do little, if anything, to police this problem – perhaps because it, like the Parked Domain, makes money off of the spurious clicks!)

TODO. If you are running on the Display Network, I recommend that you **immediately** turn it off until completing Chapter 5. You do this by going to *AdWords > Campaigns >Settings > Networks*. Change your Campaign type to "Search Network only" and uncheck the box for "Display Network."

» KEYWORD TARGETING

Keywords function very differently on the two different networks! The reason for this has to do with user behavior and what Google "knows" about the user in the different scenarios.

Scenario #1 Search. The user is pro-actively searching on Google by typing in search queries. Google "knows" **user intent** (he's looking for *cat boarding*) because it "knows" the actual search term typed into Google. For this reason, keyword matching on the Search network is **tight**: you, as the advertiser, can very tightly control when your ad appears by using the attributes of quotes (""), brackets ([]), and plus signs ("+"). (*More about this in Chapter 4*).

> **Note:** you, the advertiser, enter a "keyword trigger" such as *+cat +boarding* that Google matches to the search query entered by the searcher, *cat boarding*. Keyword matching on the Search Network is **tight**, meaning that (if you know how to correctly enter your keywords into AdWords), you can create a very tight match between what the searcher enters and when your ad displays on Google.

Scenario #2 Browse. Here, the user may be reading the *Chicago Tribune* online. He is NOT entering search terms. The most the Google knows is the content of the page he is on, but for sites like *ChicagoTribune.com, ESPN.com, USAToday.com,* etc. (all of which run Google Display Ads), Google does NOT know the user intent and is forced to compare the "page content" vs. the "keyword triggers" you as the advertiser enter into AdWords.

> **Note:** Let's take an example like the article "10 Biggest Missteps in the Bears' Decade of Decline" (**http://jmlinks.com/23p**). Here, the question for Google is, is the relevant keyword *sports* or *Bears* or *NFL* or

football or *Super Bowl*, etc., and is *Bears* a sports team or an animal (remember: Google is just a machine, not a person). Accordingly, keyword matching on the Display Network is **loosey-goosey**, that is, not at all tight, as Google has to "guess" at user interests, creating many nefarious possibilities that your ads will be placed on non-relevant websites. (Note: there are other forms of targeting your ads, such as *remarketing*, but for now we'll keep it simple).

TODO. Depending on the network you are running on, you will need to understand how to control keyword match types and adjust accordingly when Google will show your ads and on what websites.

For now, just realize that keywords drive matching on AdWords and that keywords are **tight** on the Search Network and **loosey-goosey** on the Display Network (*despite what Google indicates in its contradictory official documentation!*).

≫ BIDS AND THE QUALITY SCORE CONUNDRUM

How are ads shown on AdWords? Generally speaking, it's a cost-per-click (CPC) system, meaning that you compete against other advertisers in an online auction to "buy" the click, and you pay, if, and only if, a user clicks on your ad. Bids function the same on both the Search and Display networks; advertisers pay per click.

Let's take a simple scenario. *Jason's Cat Emporium* is competing against other cat boarding establishments to get clients who have cats and need boarding, in San Francisco as well as folks who just want cat grooming.

The Ad Auction: A Simple Model

So, imagine that Joe User goes to his computer and types into Google, *cat boarding*. At the speed of light, that query is sent to the Google algorithm in Mountain View, California, and the auctioneer (Google), says:

Incoming! I have a query, *cat boarding,* coming out of San Francisco, California. Opening bid is $1.00 for the click, do I hear $1.00?

I pipe up and say, "I'll bid $1.00 to get that click!"

The auctioneer says, "Do I hear $1.25?"

Charlie of *Charlie's Cat Boarding Inc.*, says, "Yeah! I'll bid $1.25."

The auctioneer says, "Do I hear $1.31?"

Joanie of *Joanie's Cat Boarding Inc.*, says, "Yes! I'll bid $1.31. In fact, I'll bid $2.01!"

The auctioneer says, "Do I hear $2.10?"

Silence...

The auctioneer says, "Sold! For $2.01" to Joanie's Cat Boarding.

He repeats this procedure of asking the potential advertisers for bids, having them bid against each other until he fills the top three or four slots on the Google search screen.

At the speed of light, Google then populates the Google search screen, and Joe User sees on his computer a Search Engine Results Page (or SERP), which places Joanie's ad in position #1, and positions #2, #3, and #4 on Google are populated by those who bid just a bit lower.

In reality, it's a little more complicated than this simple model because Google not only looks at advertisers' bids per click but also at their Quality Score, which is an estimation of the click thru rate for their ad (how likely it is to get more clicks) plus factors such as ad format, and the landing page experience.

VIDEO. Watch a video tutorial on how the Google bid-per-click / pay-per-click auction works by Chief Economist Hal Varian at **http://jmlinks.com/26a**.

Here's a screenshot of the Google results page for "cat boarding San Francisco" with the ad (appearing at the top), the local snack pack (appearing in the middle), and organic (appearing at the bottom) marked. In most cases, you'll see ads at the topped marked as "Ads" and the organic or free results at the bottom. For searches with a local character you'll sometimes see the "local snack pack," and for product searches such as for "red dresses," you may see product ads on the top or far right.

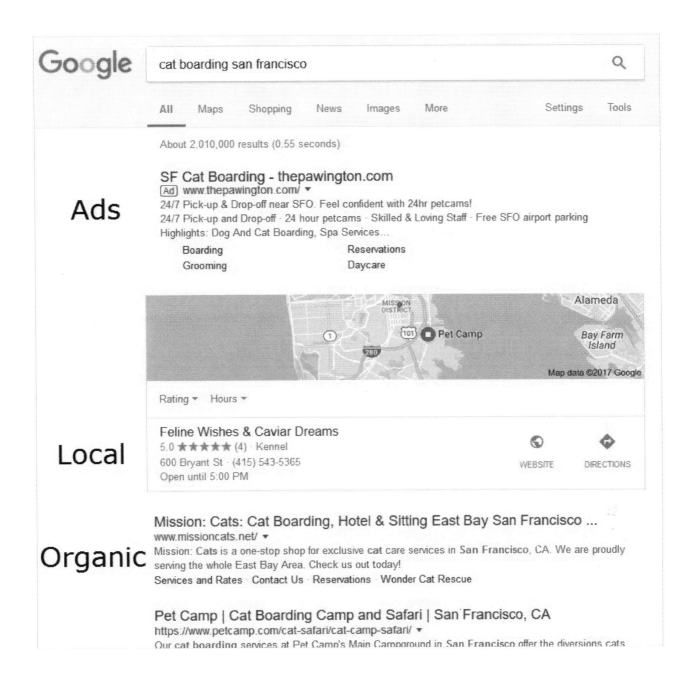

Ads

SF Cat Boarding - thepawington.com
[Ad] www.thepawington.com/ ▾
24/7 Pick-up & Drop-off near SFO. Feel confident with 24hr petcams!
24/7 Pick-up and Drop-off · 24 hour petcams · Skilled & Loving Staff · Free SFO airport parking
Highlights: Dog And Cat Boarding, Spa Services...

Boarding   Reservations
Grooming   Daycare

Local

Rating ▾   Hours ▾

Feline Wishes & Caviar Dreams
5.0 ★★★★★ (4) · Kennel
600 Bryant St · (415) 543-5365
Open until 5:00 PM

WEBSITE   DIRECTIONS

Organic

Mission: Cats: Cat Boarding, Hotel & Sitting East Bay San Francisco ...
www.missioncats.net/ ▾
Mission: Cats is a one-stop shop for exclusive cat care services in San Francisco, CA. We are proudly
serving the whole East Bay Area. Check us out today!
Services and Rates · Contact Us · Reservations · Wonder Cat Rescue

Mission: Cats: Cat Boarding, Hotel & Sitting East Bay San Francisco ...
Pet Camp | Cat Boarding Camp and Safari | San Francisco, CA
https://www.petcamp.com/cat-safari/cat-camp-safari/ ▾
Our cat boarding services at Pet Camp's Main Campground in San Francisco offer the diversions cats

Who's on Top? Ad Position

In this simple model, position #1 on Google goes to the highest bidder, position #2 to the next highest, and down to position #4. These fill the top slots. In some cases, there are additional slots at the bottom of the page, #5, #6, #7.

If or when Joe Users clicks on an ad, then that advertiser pays one penny MORE than the bid of the person just below him. So, if for example, Joanie bid $2.01 but Charlie bid just $1.10 for position #2, then Joanie would pay not $2.01 but $1.11 for that click.

That's the *simple* model. Advertisers compete against each other in the "click auction" and pay just 1¢ more than the person below them. Of course, it's more complicated than this, and Google doesn't share all the data as to what's happening behind the scenes. In fact, we are forced to trust that Google is honest and accurate with the click data, and cost per click charges; I'm not completely convinced, unfortunately, that Google is actually 100% honest on these issues, so it's best to be skeptical, measure everything, and experiment.

Here's the process from both the perspective of the searcher and of the advertiser.

1. The searcher types a **search query** into Google such as "cat boarding San Francisco."
2. Advertisers **bid** against each other to "get the click" for this search query by bidding higher to get a higher position on the page. Generally, there are three to four paid ads at the top of the page, followed by organic results (both the snack pack and organic), with a few ads at the bottom.
3. Google assembles a search engine results page (**SERP**) based on advertising (in which advertiser bid what for the click in the auction), plus organic results such as the local snack pack and regular organic results, and returns this to the searcher in the blink of an eye.
4. If a user **clicks on ads**, then whichever ad they click on pays a fee to Google called the "cost per click." (*Of course much of the time, users ignore ads and go to the organic results, which is why you must focus not only on AdWords but on SEO!*).
5. Users land on the advertiser's website and either "bounce back" to Google, or "convert" and the process repeats.

Quality Score

Ad position and the cost-per-click auction aren't quite that simple, however, because Google calculates **Quality Score**, a mysterious part of the AdWords algorithm. Basically, if you write a "better" ad (more tightly connected to the user search query), then Google will "reward" you with a lower CPC. So if Joanie bids $2.01 but her ad is poorly written (not very relevant), and Charlie bids $1.10, his ad may outrank her (be in position #1, not position #2) even though he bid less. In fact, if Joanie's ad is bad, Google may refuse to show her ad entirely.

QUALITY SCORE REWARDS ADS THAT GET CLICKS

The components of Quality Score will be discussed in Chapter 4 in more detail, but for now, just be aware that a) advertisers compete against each other in the "click auction" and "pay by the click," and b) Google rewards a better quality score with a lower cost-per-click (CPC). And, as Google skeptics, just keep in mind that we want to investigate what Quality Score really means and whether it really works the way Google says it does. Don't be fooled in AdWords by terms like "Quality Score" that sound unambiguously good for both you and for Google. "Trust but verify," as President Reagan once said about the Soviet Union.

The Quality Score Conundrum

There is, however, a conundrum in Quality Score which Google does not explain. Remember that Google gets paid *by the click*, while you make money *by the conversion*, which is not the same thing! So, if you write an ad that says "Cheap Cat Boarding" or even "Free Cat Boarding" or "Free Cat Boarding Plus Free Pizza for Owners" you will a) get a lot of clicks, b) improve your Quality Score, and c) pay less per click.

Google will be VERY happy!

But you will get a lot of cheap customers who are coming just because you're cheap (and you provide free pizza), that is few conversions and/or conversions from people who are not willing to pay full price for your quality cat boarding services.

The conundrum is that you are competing against advertisers who may not understand this, who follow Google's official playbook, and whose ads (*for free pizza and free cat boarding*) "crowd out" your more honest, more relevant ads.

You are forced to overbid just to stay in the game!

We'll return to this problem in Chapter 4, but for now just realize that advertisers "pay by the click" on Google and that there is a tension inherent in Quality Score between your interests (*to get the conversion*) and Google's interest (*to get the click*) plus you are often competing against a few dumb advertisers who think it's all about clicks and thereby hijack users to their pages with ads that overpromise, thus stupidly bidding up the costs for everyone else.

The system is far less perfect than Google makes it out to be.

Minimum Bids

In addition, Google has minimum bids which mean even if you are the ONLY advertiser bidding on a specific keyword phrase, you can't just bid one cent for the click. There is a non-published "minimum bid" which you must find out through trial and error. Despite what Google officially says, you don't exactly pay just .01 above the person below you, and you can't just optimize for clicks to improve your so-called Quality Score.

Bear with me on this, as we'll return to bid strategy in Chapter 4. For now, just realize that generally speaking, you bid per click against other advertisers, and you pay just .01 above the advertiser below you. All of this is mediated by Quality Score, with Google rewarding advertisers that write ads that get a lot of clicks.

» WHY USE ADWORDS?

At this point, you may be wondering, *"Gosh, why use AdWords at all? It sounds very complicated and seems to have quite a few 'gotchas' inserted there to take my money."*

I understand that frustration, but (*back to our analogy of a trip to Brazil*), there are many wonderful things to see, do, and take advantage of in the country of AdWordsLandia, if you know where to look, and know how to avoid the bad neighborhoods and cultural gotchas that can cause trouble.

> **VIDEO.** Watch a video from Google on defining your goals for advertising on AdWords **http://jmlinks.com/26c**.

Here's a rundown of reasons why AdWords should have a place in your online marketing strategy:

1. **Time to Market**. AdWords can get your company, product, or service to the top of Google, quickly. You can literally set up an ad campaign in just a few hours, and be up and running on Google. This allows you to react quickly to market events, and get your message out and up in a much, much faster way than search engine optimization(SEO) which takes considerable time and effort.

2. **Geotargeting**. AdWords is very effective at targeting consumers in just a specific area. You can target ONLY people in San Jose, California, for example, and you can target people in San Jose with one ad and people in Tulsa, Oklahoma, with another ad. Indeed, you can also show your ad only during certain times of the day or week through scheduling.

3. **Short Tail Queries**. You may be able to rank via SEO for a very specific search such as *quality cat boarding in the Mission district, San Francisco*, but be unable to rank for a *short tail* query such as *cat boarding*. Using AdWords, you can strategically advertise on short tail queries that you do not rank for via SEO. Combined with geotargeting, this can be a very powerful complement to search engine optimization.

4. **Keyword Broad Match**. While SEO works well on very focused keywords, AdWords can get your ads to show on broader, adjacent keywords. For example, you can combine a geotarget (people in San Francisco) with an "educational search term" such as "how to groom a cat" to showcase your cat grooming services. You can also get detailed reporting in AdWords to identify relevant keyword targets for your SEO that you cannot get in any other way. When used with skill and caution, AdWords can get your message to a broader audience than pure SEO.

5. **Keyword Research**. Google no longer provides detailed keyword data to organic or SEO users, but it does provide keyword data to AdWords advertisers. By advertising, you can get invaluable research into the actual keywords used by users and their behavior "after the click," which you can feed back into your AdWords and/or SEO strategy.

6. **Mobile Phone Targeting**. It's no secret that people spend more and more time on their mobile phones. The screen is very small, and Google has "crowded out" the free listings by pushing them down with ads. Using AdWords, you can effectively advertise on mobile phones, only, again adding a powerful complement to an effective SEO strategy. You can turn "off" AdWords on the desktop (where you rank well in the organic / SEO results), for example, and turn "on" AdWords on the mobile phone (where you rank poorly in the organic / SEO results).

7. **Remarketing**. Using *remarketing* (explained in Chapter 5), you can "follow" your customers around the Internet as they go to sites like *YouTube, Gmail, Chicago Tribune, New York Times*, etc., showing and reshowing them relevant ads about your product or service. Remarketing is very powerful for products or services with long sales cycles like *cruises to Latin America, choosing a tax CPA,* or even *applying to law schools.*

8. **Browsing / Interrupt**. While SEO works if, and only if, the person is pro-actively searching Google, AdWords can show your ads through the Google Display Network and YouTube to people who are NOT pro-actively looking for your product. You can "interrupt" their experience with ads on YouTube, or get your ads on relevant blogs and news sites via the Google Display Network.

I like to think of SEO as the art and science of getting a company to the top of Google for free and, as the world's cheapest man, I ALWAYS seek to get as much as I can get for free from Google. Then, using tactics such as geotargeting, short tail keyword matches, mobile phones or remarketing, I blend in AdWords for a killer online marketing strategy.

*It's not AdWords OR SEO. It's AdWords ** **AND** ** SEO!*

I hope that this seven-point list has fired up your enthusiasm for AdWords!

⏩ ELEMENTS OF ADS ON ADWORDS

Remember that AdWords is two primary networks, Google Search and the Google Display Network. With that in mind, let's overview the elements to ads. What do ads look like on each network?

The Search Network

Ads on Google have the following components:

Headline 1 – 30 characters

Headline 2 – 30 characters

Description – 80 characters

Path ("Display URL") – 15 characters each

Here's a screenshot of a simple ad triggered by motorcycle insurance:

Motorcycle Insurance CA - Lowest Rates, $6/Month - mis-insurance.com
Ad sr22.mis-**insurance**.com/ ▾
Free Quotes. Speak To Live Agent. Print Your ID Card Online

Ad Extensions

In addition to the headline, description, and path, ads on Google can also have "extensions." These can be:

Sitelinks – these are blue-highlighted bits of text that can appear below an ad, and link to specific subsections of your website such as "contact us" or "cat grooming," etc.

Callouts – these are non-clickable text elements that can appear below an ad, usually meant to "call out" something special such as "Valentine's Day Specials" or "ask about our kitty services".

Structured Snippets – you select a predefined header like "Product" or "Service category" and then add callouts to specific subsections of your website.

Call extensions – these allow your phone number to appear in ads.

Message extensions – these appear on mobile phone ads and allow customers to text message you directly from the ad.

Location – this extension type allows users to see your store's physical address.

Affiliate location – similar to the above.

Price extensions – allow users to browse products and prices in an ad, and then click directly to them on your website.

App extensions – allow you to link from your ad to your mobile app for download and installation.

Reviews – this extension type allows you to pull reviews from third party websites and thereby enable review stars on your ads.

Promotion Extension – use this extension like a callout extension to "shout out" a custom offer like a coupon or discount.

Google has a new type of extension called "**Automated Extensions**" which occur automatically when Google decides to features something like a specific page on your website or a phone number. To read the official Google help file on ad extensions, visit **http://jmlinks.com/23q**. To read about the newer Automated Extensions, visit **http://jmlinks.com/39p**.

Here's a screenshot of an ad with clickable sitelink extensions:

GEICO Motorcycle Insurance - Quoting is Fast and Free - geico.com
Ad www.geico.com/ ▾ (888) 475-3540
Bike and accessories coverage for the extras that make your bike your own.
Free Quotes · 75+ Years of Savings · 24/7 Service & Claims · Mobile App
Ratings: Selection 9.5/10 - Ease of purchase 9.5/10 - Service 9/10 - Website 8.5/10

Get a Quote   BIG Savings
Switch & Save   Save 15% or More

And here's a screenshot of an ad with a location extension and stars (coming from their Google reviews):

DeVry Accounting Degree - DeVry.edu
Ad www.devry.edu/ ▼ (855) 604-8442
Year-Round, Accelerated Classes. Earn Your Degree At DeVry, Get Info
Degrees in Growing Fields · Merit-Based Scholarships · Locations Nationwide
Degree programs: Accounting, Business Administration, Business Management, Technical Management
♦ 6600 Dumbarton Cr, Fremont, CA - 4.3 ★★★★★ 6 reviews

Notice how DeVry has added their phone number of 855-604-8442 as a call extension, and how the location extension shows their address.

And here's a screenshot with a review extension, again getting the advertiser those nifty, eye-catching stars:

Warehouse Industrial Fans - In Stock. Ships Today - uline.com
Ad www.uline.com/Warehouse-Fans ▼
4.6 ★★★★★ rating for uline.com
ULINE - Over 31,000 Items in Stock. Huge Catalog! Same Day Shipping.
Fast Delivery · 11 Locations · 31,000+ Products
Ratings: Shipping 9.5/10 - Quality 8.5/10 - Website 8.5/10 - Selection 8.5/10 - Add-on services 8/10

| Floor Fans | Pedestal Fans |
| Wall Mount Fans | Drum Fans |

Notice how this ad has a display URL that contains a keyword (*Warehouse-Fans*), as well as call out extensions and structured snippet extensions.

The Display Network

Ads on the Display Network can be text and appear similar to the above. Or they can be graphic images. You can either upload your own or use Google's "Responsive Ad" tool to have it pull images from your website and create a cornucopia of possible image sizes for your ad. Here, you can run ads that are

Dynamic Ads – rich media ads that match the device / format a person is on.

Lightbox Ads – interactive ads that can allow users to pull needed information right from the ad.

Video ads – ads that display a video about your company, product, or service.

Animated ads – ads that are images that may, or may not, be animated.

Gmail ads – ads that appear in the promotions tab on Gmail.

To read the official Google help file on how to create "responsive ads" for the Display Network, visit **http://jmlinks.com/23r**. Note that if you are not running on the Display Network, then you can ignore these ads format as they are not available on Google Search. Also be aware that YouTube has specific ad requirements and formats; you can read the official Google help file on YouTube ads at **http://jmlinks.com/23s**. Suffice it to say at this point that there are many more formatting options for ads on the Google Display Network than on the Search Network.

» AdWords Organization

AdWords is a hierarchy. Remember that Google is a company founded by, and run by, engineers. These are stereotypically the guys with the pocket protectors, the over-organized desks, and the Sheldon Cooper personality types that need to always "sit in their spot." (To learn more about Sheldon Cooper and ponder whether this personality type is overrepresented in the Googleplex, visit **http://jmlinks.com/23t**, but we digress).

AdWords is a hierarchy! The more organized you are, the better you will do!

Accordingly, you will get your best performance by understanding and following AdWords strict hierarchical rules:

Account. This is the master category and contains your email login, password, and billing information. I recommend that you set up two-step verification (**http://jmlinks.com/23v**) for your AdWords account, as thieves target AdWords accounts because there is money to be stolen!

Campaigns. Think of a campaign as a "bucket" that holds your budget, bid strategy (but not your actual bids), network choice (Search vs. Display), geotarget, device target (mobile, desktop, tablet), and a few other odds and ends such as scheduling.

Ad Groups. Groups are the workhorses of AdWords and should reflect your product or service categories and tightly correspond to your core keywords. Bids are also set at the group level, or at the interrelated keyword level. An example of group organization would be "cat boarding" vs. "cat grooming"; different customer needs create different search queries and should be reflected in corresponding, unique AdWords groups

Cross-Views in AdWords: Confusion Alert!

AdWords is a hierarchy at a structural level. However, you can "view" across the structure in different ways. For example, you can log in to your Account, click on the "Keywords" tab and view ALL the keywords across ALL the groups of your account. However, "Keywords" live at the group level, only, so any edits that you make impact them at that level.

Imagine, for example, a glass building called "Account," that had two floors, called "Campaigns" and "Groups." At any moment you could see "through" the building in any direction, but, for example, the "budget information" would "live" on the "Campaign floor." While you could be on the "group" floor and "see" the budget, you couldn't touch it (or edit it), without moving to the "Campaign floor."

AdWords is like a glass building. You can "see" many things in many different ways, but you can only manage or edit them at the correct level. For example:

   Budget can be edited only at the Campaign level.

   Ads can be edited only at the Ad Group level.

   Bids can be edited only at the Group or keyword level

   Geotargeting can be edited only at the Campaign level

      and so on and so forth...

This is confusing to people as you can "view" things in AdWords in ways that do NOT reflect the structural organization. I recommend you ask yourself "what level does this live at?" when you're having a problem editing something, and go to that level by clicking on the appropriate tab.

VIDEO. Watch an official video tutorial on best practices for AdWords account organization at **http://jmlinks.com/23u**.

At this point, don't freak out about the organizational issues at AdWords. Like working in a big, fancy glass building in San Francisco, over time, the organization will make sense to you and become second nature.

» GETTING ONLINE HELP WITH ADWORDS

My companion *AdWords Toolbook* has a cornucopia of resources on AdWords, including tools and help documentation. That said, here are the official resources where you can "ask a question" of AdWords.

Help. Help is hidden in AdWords under the "Question Mark Icon" in the top right of the screen. Click on it and then select "Get Help."

Live chat and Email Help. These can be found in the "help" section as indicated above.

Phone Support. Click on the "Question Mark Icon," and you should see a phone number. In the United States, the number is 866-246-6453. Live technical support is available 9 am – 8 pm Eastern Time.

You can also access the AdWords help files at **https://support.google.com/adwords**. You can post questions to the Google AdWords Community at **https://www.en.advertisercommunity.com/**. Throughout, be aware that Google has a vested interest in your spending MORE (not less) money on AdWords, so the technical support at all levels can be a bit salesy.

▶▶ DELIVERABLE: ADWORDS STRATEGY WORKSHEET

The **DELIVERABLE** for this chapter focuses on the Big Picture. Why are you interested in advertising on AdWords? Which network (Search or Display) makes the most sense for your products or services?

For the **worksheet**, go to **https://www.jm-seo.org/workbooks** (click on "AdWords Workbook 2018," enter the code 'adwords18' to register if you have not already done so), and click on the link to the "AdWords Strategy" worksheet.

2

ADWORDS GOTCHAS

Google AdWords is full of "gotchas," misleading elements in the platform that can cause you to advertise on the wrong keywords, run on websites you don't really like, pay more for clicks than necessary, and otherwise make your advertising inefficient and expensive. By their very nature, these gotchas are hidden to the average user. Note: we will circle back to the gotchas in the Chapters to come, but if you are currently advertising on Google, I strongly recommend that you either completely **stop all advertising** until you have completed this Workbook, or at least until after you have read this Chapter. After all, the first principle of using advertising to *make* money is to NOT *waste* money on advertising!

Let's get started!

TODO LIST:

>> Understand the AdWords Contradiction

>> Gotcha #1: AdWords Alternatives

>> Gotcha #2: Bad Keyword Match Types

>> Gotcha#3: The Google Display Network

>> Gotcha #4 Conversions Across Devices

>>>> Deliverable: An AdWords Gotcha Checkup

>> UNDERSTAND THE ADWORDS CONTRADICTION

AdWords is a multi-billion dollar source of revenue for Google. It's how Google makes the lion's share of its money, to the tune of 90% or more in any given year. In 2016, for example, Google generated about $89.5 billion in revenue, with about 90% coming from advertising both on Google itself and on its AdSense network. (See **http://jmlinks.com/39m**). AdWords, in short, is how Google funds all those incredible engineer dreams like self-driving cars, dreams that often *lose* Google money. And – very significantly – Google does not make its money off of consumers directly, nor directly off of providing the "most relevant" results for any given search query (despite what the average person believes).

Google, The Click, and The Conversion

At a structural level, there is a *tension* or even a *contradiction* between you (*the advertiser*) and Google (the *publisher*):

> Google is paid by the *click*; accordingly, Google wants ads that create lots of *clicks*.
>
> You make money by the *conversion* (usually an e-Commerce sale or a sales lead via a web form on your website); you want ads that create a lot of *conversions*.
>
> Google wants you to spend a lot of money on AdWords; Google wants you to *maximize your spend*.
>
> You want to spend, as little as possible or as effectively as possible, to *maximize your ROAS* or *Return on Ad Spend*, that is, the profit you make from advertising efficiently.

The focus of Google is to get users to click on ads and to get advertisers to pay for those clicks. Everything else at Google is a means to this end.

Now, don't get me wrong. It's not that Google is totally evil and nefarious. Google is just a for-profit business, doing what for-profit businesses do, that is – maximizing profit. But, despite what mountains of Google webinars, help literature, AdWords rep's, articles in the newspaper, and others will tell you, it's not true that Google has your best interest at heart or even the best interests of web searchers. Indeed, you might do better to think of Google not as a "search engine" but as a "**click engine**" or a "**profit engine**," Google's not yours.

Your relationship to Google is a business one: it can be win/win, but it can also be win/lose.

GOOGLE GETS PAID BY THE CLICK; YOU, BY THE CONVERSION

Let's take an example. Suppose you are selling "Motorcycle Insurance" as an independent insurance rep in San Francisco, California. You want to attract customers who need to buy motorcycle insurance, and you know that many of them will turn first to Google, and type into Google search queries such as the following:

motorcycle insurance

motorcycle insurance agency

insurance agents that sell insurance for motorcycles

motorcycle insurance quote

motorcycle insurance cost

cheap motorcycle insurance

motorcycle insurance for Harleys

Etc.

You can view this cornucopia of search queries by using the free SERPS.com keyword discovery tool at **http://jmlinks.com/29g**. Just enter the phrase "motorcycle insurance" into the Keyword(s) box, type in the *Captcha*, and hit *search*. Next click on the "Volume" column to sort by volume. Ignore the branded searches that contain vendor names such as "Geico" or "Progressive" and browse down the list. You should see something like:

Keyword	Volume	CPC
motorcycle insurance	22,200	$24.47
motorcycle insurance quote	5,400	$20.46
cheap motorcycle insurance	3,600	$17.35
best motorcycle insurance	1,900	$23.47
motorcycle insurance rates	1,000	$15.89
cheapest motorcycle insurance	1,900	$18.48

The cost per click as indicated by the tool is approximately $24.47 per click – meaning if a user clicks on your ad for "motorcycle insurance," you, as an advertiser, are going to pay Google – on average - $24.47 per click. As an advertiser, you are highly motivated that the person who "clicks" is also likely to "convert," that is, become a paying customer. (Note: Because Google makes money by the click alone – and not by whether or not that person becomes a paying customer – Google is indifferent as to whether they actually convert – Google loves clicks and clicks and clicks at $24.47 per click!).

Now, looking at the tool, you'll see that many people type into Google the phrase:

cheap motorcycle insurance

And some really cheap people type in *cheapest motorcycle insurance* - 1,900 cheapskate searchers per month according to the tool.

But it stands to reason that a person who types in *cheap motorcycle insurance* is likely to be poor, or at least value conscious, and less likely to buy and/or less likely to buy a premium policy. Looking to the future, you might want "cheap" to be a "negative keyword" (which we'll explain later), but just understand a negative keyword to be hidden instructions to Google:

If they enter the word *cheap*, then Google, please do NOT show my ad.

Similarly, Google would like you to advertise in a broad geographic area, perhaps not just the city of San Francisco, but the entire Bay Area or even all of California. That will generate the most clicks (and most revenue for Google). But, it stands to reason, that persons closest to your insurance agency may be more likely to perceive you as "local" and therefore actually buy. Google wants a wide geographic net, and you want to at least research whether a wide (or a narrow) geography will generate more conversions, at a lower cost. Indeed, let's say that you realize that Harley-Davidson owners make the most profitable customers, and you might want to advertise only on phrases such as:

motorcycle insurance for Harleys

Harley insurance

Harley-Davidson insurance

Harley Davidson motorcycle insurance

Insurance for Harley bikes

etc.

You might decide that you want to be very narrow, in other words, targeting only people who are searching for Harley insurance, and only within a range of 10 miles from your face-to-face insurance agency . *Narrow may be better for you than the broad reach that Google tends to imply is better.*

Google Rewards Ads that Get Clicks

Similarly, if you look at an ad on Google, it has two lines of text, a URL and perhaps a few extensions such as your phone number or other text lines.

Here's a screenshot of an actual ad for "motorcycle insurance:"

GEICO Motorcycle Insurance - Get a Free Quote Online - GEICO.com
Ad www.geico.com/ ▾
Get a free cycle quote in 15 minutes or less! Discover how much you could save.
Insurance coverage: Auto, Motorcycle, Boat, Renters
Ratings: Selection 9.5/10 - Ease of purchase 9.5/10 - Website 9/10 - Claim handling 9/10

Get a Quote   Save 15% or More
BIG Savings   Switch & Save

Imagine that that ad said "Cheap Motorcycle Insurance – Lowest Rates Around" or even better it said, "Free Motorcycle Insurance," or even better it said "Free Motorcycle Insurance Plus a Free Pizza Just for Clicking," what would happen?

You would drive up the clicks (making Google more money).

You would, however, attract many "tire kicker" customers interested in only "free" or "cheap" motorcycle insurance, or worse "free pizza" thereby reducing your conversions.

Google would be happy. No, Google would be more than happy. Google would be ecstatic! Indeed, Google touts a metric called Quality Score (**http://jmlinks.com/25x**), and Google would "reward" your ad with a high "Quality Score" because of it high click thru rate. What could possibly be bad about a high quality score?

You, however, would not be so happy as your AdWords advertising cost would go up (*more clicks*) and your *conversions* would go down (fewer quality people buying).

Google wants you to advertise on lots of keywords.

Google wants you to advertise on broad geographies.

Google wants you to write ad copy that says "free" or "free pizza" and "free beer."

Now, to be fair, this is somewhat of an exaggeration. If you read the instructions to AdWords, Google does point out that you should create *relevant* ads on *relevant* keywords, but they bury this tension between "clicks" and "conversions" enough that most people, even many advanced practitioners, and ad agency types, are unaware of this fundamental tension between Google and its advertisers.

Many people mistakenly assume that AdWords <u>for the advertiser and not Google</u> is about getting **clicks** when really AdWords <u>for the advertiser and not Google</u> is about getting **conversions**. Indeed, one of the more popular books on AdWords says right on the cover, "Double your web traffic overnight," which could be completely useless when what you really want is to "Double your conversions" or "Increase the profit from your ad spend."

That doesn't sound so sexy on a book cover, however.

The Google Propaganda Machine

In our Internet-infused times, you may have noticed a steady uptick in fake facts, fake news, and information of questionable validity. This is true also with respect to AdWords. With billions at stake, Google has a very loud propaganda machine explaining the benefits of AdWords (to be fair, so does Facebook, Twitter, and even Snapchat about advertising on their platforms). If you call into AdWords "tech support" or allow AdWords to "optimize" your account, you may find a strong preference for tactics that expand your reach, increase your clicks, and grow your budget over tactics that increase the effectiveness of your ads as measured by conversions. The Google propaganda machine, unfortunately, tilts towards you spending more money to get more clicks.

There's lip service paid to the importance of relevance and conversions, but most of the emphasis at Google is to a) get you to advertise, and b) get you to expand your budget and your ad copy to encourage clicks. In fact, a cynic would say that much of the keyword, conversion, and placement data is hidden in AdWords so that advertisers "trust" Google to be running ads in their interest as opposed to actually validating their performance with real data.

For an example, there's even a tool inside AdWords called Bid Simulator. Go to *Campaigns > Ad Group* and then hover your mouse over the Default Max CPC. You'll see a little box with a squiggly arrow in it. Here's a screenshot from:

Click on the squiggly box, and AdWords will pop up a simulation, and (*surprise, surprise, surprise* like Gomer Pyle said on the TV show), it will generally encourage you to *increase* your bid per click (often dramatically) to get just a few more clicks. You can also drill down at the keyword level and do the same process at the keyword level.

Here's a screenshot after clicking the squiggly box at the keyword level:

Ad group bid simulator: ▮▮▮▮▮▮▮

Explore how your bid can impact your Search traffic, then apply any changes to your ad group. Learn more

Simulate: ● Leaving any keyword-specific bids ⑦   ○ Applying bid to all keywords ⑦

Max. CPC	Clicks	Cost	Impr.	Top Impr.	Conv.
○ $16.70	259	$2,440.00	2,983	795	15
○ $13.40	249	$2,040.00	2,915	696	15
○ $11.50	235	$1,650.00	2,838	603	14
○ $9.58	219	$1,300.00	2,730	485	13
◉ $8.01 (current)	197	$1,030.00	2,593	366	12
○ $6.70	166	$725.00	2,119	234	10
○ $5.79	133	$518.00	1,744	176	9
○ $ Set a different bid					

So, Google would like me to increase my bid from $8.01 to $16.70 per click, to gain three more conversions at a cost of $1410 or $470 per extra conversion. Is this good for me, or good for Google? (That depends).

You have to know what you're doing and know that Google is tilting the emphasis towards clicks to see the problem here. Indeed, most beginner advertisers don't even enable conversions and may not even see that the cost per conversion is an issue.

> *Google tilts you to think "get more clicks," when I want you to think "get more conversions."*

Even worse, in my experience, there is often not a straight line relationship between increasing your bid per click, getting more impressions, getting more clicks, and getting more conversions. Sometimes if you bid *lower*, you actually get *more* impressions and *more* clicks, and even *more* conversions – in direct contradiction to Google's public help files!

Now, please don't think I am an extremist and think AdWords is a scam. I'm not, and it isn't.

I wouldn't be writing a book about AdWords if I didn't see the value in online advertising. AdWords can be incredible! But with an eye to the tension between Google's "hunger for clicks" and your own "hunger for conversions," we can learn – together - how to maximize our AdWords investment.

> *Just remember – always remember – that Google makes its money on clicks, and you make your money on conversions.*

With this tension in the back of our minds, let's dive into the four "Gotchas" lurking inside AdWords.

» Gotcha #1: AdWords Alternatives

If you go on a Chevy lot, the car dealer will try to sell you a Chevy. He isn't likely to explain that a Toyota might be better for your needs, nor that using Uber or Lyft might be an even more effective way to secure your transportation.

Similarly, if you reach out to Google, you'll find that AdWords is the best alternative for any Internet marketing needs. Better than –

SEO or Search Engine Optimization, the art and science of getting your company to the top of Google for free. (See my *SEO Fitness Workbook* at **http://jmlinks.com/seo**).

Email Marketing or using email services like Constant Contact, Mail Chimp, or Aweber to build a following of interested customers.

Social Media Marketing, or using free marketing on Facebook, LinkedIn, Twitter, Snapchat and other social media networks (See my *Social Media Workbook* at **http://jmlinks.com/smm**).

Facebook Advertising. Paying to advertise on Facebook, the world's largest social media network.

YouTube Advertising. Paying to advertise on YouTube, Google's subsidiary focused on video.

Twitter Advertising. Paying to advertise on Twitter.

Review marketing. Working hard to get positive customer reviews on sites like Yelp, Google reviews, eBay, etc.

Optimizing on Amazon, eBay, or other specific websites. Some industries (e.g., books) are dominated by certain websites (e.g., Amazon), and Google advertising will do little, if anything, to influence them.

Doing Nothing at All and relying on word of mouth.

Gotcha #1 is to "**fail to consider alternatives.**" AdWords may not generate the highest ROI for your marketing investment. Generally speaking, SEO will usually far, far outperform AdWords in terms of ROI, while other tactics like social media marketing or advertising on Facebook, Twitter, or YouTube can be cost-competitive in many instances. Indeed, word of mouth and eWom (electronic word of mouth) will nearly always outperform every other marketing vehicle. So before you use AdWords, or simultaneously to your use of AdWords, be sure to maximize every other alternative that may generate a higher ROI.

Usually, a smart marketing effort will have some blood, sweat, tears, and budget in SEO, some in AdWords, some in WOM / eWOM, some in free social media marketing efforts, and some in other advertising venues such as Facebook or LinkedIn.

AdWords has a very loud and very powerful propaganda machine (compared, for example, with SEO or email marketing), but that loudness does not mean it generates the highest ROI for you as a small business. It just means that it has a lot of Google dollars behind it!

TODO. Consider all online publicity alternatives, both free and paid, and allocate your budget (both time and money) accordingly. Usually, you want a mix of more than one advertising or marketing vehicle, looking for the highest ROI across media.

» Gotcha#2: Bad Keyword Match Types

If you are advertising on AdWords, a very common problem is Gotcha #2, "bad match types" for your keywords. We will discuss this in detail in Chapter 4 on the Google Search Network, but for now, let's discuss this basic gotcha.

We'll assume that you've done at least a little keyword research and that you understand you want to run your ads on keyword queries that are "likely" to be your customers and "likely" to be those customers near the moment of purchase.

A San Francisco insurance agent, for example, would set his geotarget to San Francisco, California, and run on keywords such as:

> *motorcycle insurance*
>
> *insurance for Harley-Davidsons*

And not

> *motorcycle clubs* (too broad)
>
> *motorcycle* (too broad!)
>
> *insurance* (too broad!)

In addition, you need to understand **keyword match types** in AdWords.

When you input keywords into Google AdWords to tell Google when to run your ad, be sure to enter either a plus "+" sign, a "quote", or a bracket "[" in front of your keywords. If, for example, you want to run on the keywords "motorcycle insurance," these should be entered into AdWords as follows:

> *"motorcycle insurance"*
>
> *+motorcycle +insurance*
>
> *[motorcycle insurance]*

That is, phrase match, modified broad, or exact match. NEVER EVER enter just the words as for example:

motorcycle insurance

Despite the official Google help explanation (**http://jmlinks.com/23d**), using broad match (*just the words, without quotation marks, plus signs, or brackets*) can produce many poor matches. In this example, Google might substitute

"scooter" for "motorcycle"

so that your ad would show for

scooter insurance

which you may, or may not offer. It can be worse. For example, a keyword target entered as just *cat insurance* (no quotes, plus signs, or brackets) can end up running on search queries like *pet insurance* or even *dog insurance* generating lots of clicks but few sales or sales inquiries.

In addition, you want to pay attention to words that mean different things (e.g., "Joint repair," meaning I need a new kneecap or "joint repair" meaning I need a new CV joint for my Toyota.)

Negative Keywords

Another keyword problem is a failure to identify and input "negative keywords" that indicate people are just looking for free or cheap stuff, like the words "free" or "cheap." After all, someone looking for "free cat boarding" isn't exactly the same type of customer as someone looking for "luxury cat boarding," yet if you enter into AdWords just:

cat boarding

no "+" sign, no "quote" mark and no "[]" brackets and no negative keywords like *-free, -cheap,* you are saying to the AdWords bartender, "get me a whiskey, any old whiskey will do." Run me on

cat boarding

discount cat boarding

free cat boarding

cheap cat boarding

cat boarding for cat owners who don't care about their cats

etc.

Specificity, not trust, is what you need in your communications with AdWords. So you want to specify the correct match type and the negative keywords.

TODO If you are currently running on broad match, I highly recommend you go through your keywords and immediately add at least plus "+" signs in front of all your keywords! If you can easily identify obvious negative keywords, add those into your Ad Groups at once.

Find Out Your Actual Keywords

To see the keywords you are actually running, click into an Ad Group (Right Column) and then click on the blue name of your Ad Group. Next, click *Search Terms* and then *Search Terms* again.

Here's a screenshot showing the actual search terms entered:

	Search term	Match type	Added/Excluded
☐			
	Total: Search terms		
☐	social media marketing books	Exact match	✓ Added
☐	best social media marketing books	Exact match (close variant)	None
☐	best books on social media marketing	Exact match	✓ Added
☐	best social media marketing books 2017	Phrase match	None

SEARCH KEYWORDS   NEGATIVE KEYWORDS   SEARCH TERMS ▼

These are the *actual* terms people typed into Google, and in the column marked "clicks," you can see if they clicked (and you paid for those clicks); if you have conversions enabled, you can also see which keywords led to conversions.

- If all these terms make sense as relevant to your business, you're in OK shape.
- If, however, you see terms that are way off the mark, you have a problem caused by "Gotcha #2," *bad match types.*

Regardless, immediately tighten up your keyword matches by adding quotation marks, plus signs, and/or brackets. You can also add **negative keywords** if there are terms that clearly designate a non-customer. You want to be in control of your keywords, not Google. (More about this in Chapter 4 on the Search Network).

» GOTCHA#3: THE GOOGLE DISPLAY NETWORK

"Gotcha #3" is the Google Display Network or GDN. Many people do not realize that AdWords runs on two very different networks, the *Search Network* (primarily Google but also search-driven sites like Yelp or Comcast) and the *Display Network* (a network of sites such as YouTube and Gmail but also blogs, parked domains, web portals and many nefarious sites that seem to exist primarily to steal your money).

THE DISPLAY NETWORK IS PROBLEMATIC

You can watch an inaccurate and salesy pitch by Google on the Google Display Network at **http://jmlinks.com/23e**. This is akin to watching a movie trailer about Hollywood's latest horror movie or an introductory video on the latest Ford Mustang by Ford. It is NOT an independent, objective explanation of how the Google Display Network works! It is a sales piece!

The problem is that the GDN contains many badly matched and even fraudulent sites that exist solely to capture clicks and take your ad dollars. If you are not experienced, DO NOT RUN on the Google Display Network!

Default Setting: On

Unfortunately, the default setting on Google is to run on both search and display. In AdWords' New Interface, Google has made it even harder for inexperienced advertisers to see the Google Display Network when they set up a new campaign.

When you click the blue "+" sign to set up a new campaign, you'll first see:

Select a campaign type ⑦

Search Network	Display Network	Shopping	Video	Universal App
Reach customers interested in your product or service with text ads	Run different kinds of ads across the web	Promote your products with Shopping ads	Reach and engage viewers on YouTube and across the web	Drive app installs across Google's networks

And then you'll have to be very careful to "opt out" of the Display Network as it rears its ugly head at various points in the setup process. Here's a screenshot showing where you have to pro-actively uncheck a box to "opt out" of the Display Network:

Search Network

Ads can appear near Google Search results and other Google sites when people search for terms that are relevant to your keywords

☑ Include Google search partners ⑦

Display Network

Expand your reach by showing ads to relevant customers as they browse sites, videos, and apps across the internet

☑ Include Google Display Network ⑦

If you are running on the GDN without understanding it, you may be running on many terrible placements up to and including fraudulent sites that do nothing more than generate spurious clicks and cost you money.

TODO. Turn off the Google Display Network and run only on the Search Network.

To disable the Google Display Network, click into a Campaign, and then click *Settings* on the left column. Next, find the *Networks* tab in the middle of the page. Click the downward chevron to expand the box, until you see:

Make sure that the box under Display Network is unchecked; I also recommend you uncheck *Google Search partners* as well, though this is not as unambiguously terrible. Google has rigged AdWords very much to default you into the Display Network, so dig in, find your settings, and run only on the Search Network, until you pro-actively decide that the GDN has value for you.

» GOTCHA#4: CONVERSIONS ACROSS DEVICES

You may have heard that Google is now "mobile first." Google believes that because most search activity occurs on mobile devices like phones and tablets (vs. desktop computers), everyone should run full blast on mobile devices. However, the fact that a lot of click volume occurs on mobile phones does not mean that the best conversion rates occur on mobile phones. (Remember: Google gets paid off of *clicks*, and you get paid off of *conversions*). It depends on your business.

For some businesses, it is highly desirable to reach consumers on their mobile devices, getting the click from Google, and then getting a conversion on a mobile device on your website. But for many businesses, the mobile experience isn't very good, and many customers click from Google on a mobile device to your website, only to bounce and fail to convert.

VERIFY ADS ON PHONES ACTUALLY CONVERT

"Gotcha #4," accordingly, occurs when you're running on phone, tablets, and desktops when you may be converting far better on only one of these platforms. In my experience, especially for complicated products like insurance, CPA service, hair transplants and the like, generally, the desktop conversion rate far outperforms that of the mobile phone or tablet. Your **TODO** here is to verify that your mobile conversions are as strong as your desktop conversions and turn each on or off, or adjust your bids up or down, accordingly.

The default setting is to run on –

Computers – PCs and MACS on the desktop.

Tablets with full browsers – iPad and Android tablets

Mobile devices with full browsers – mobile phones like iPhones and Android phones

You can see your impressions and clicks across devices by selecting a Campaign (or drilling down one more level into an Ad Group), and then clicking on *Devices*. You can then toggle between Campaigns and Ad Groups by clicking the blue *Level* link at the top.

You may not have conversions turned "on" yet. If not, you may show zero conversions across all device types. You can also go to Google Analytics (**https://www.google.com/analytics**), then click on Segments, next turn on "Mobile Traffic" and "Tablet and Desktop Traffic." You can then compare your mobile phone traffic to your desktop traffic and look at the relative bounce rate and conversions.

Here's a screenshot, for example, that shows that cost per conversion is far worse on mobile phones and tablets vs. desktop computers:

Device	Impr. ↓	Cost	Clicks	Conversions	Cost / conv.
Mobile phones	10,047	$1,492.79	321	20.00	$74.64
Computers	8,545	$1,881.86	276	35.00	$53.77
Tablets	1,437	$428.90	55	5.00	$85.78
Total: Account	96,006	$4,368.64	834	60.00	$72.81

Level: **Campaign; C...**

In this example, we'd then want to de-emphasize our ads on mobile phones and emphasize our ads on desktop computers. Despite the Google hype about mobile, we're doing better on the desktop!

A Gut Check

Note: if you don't have conversion tracking turned on, or don't understand. Don't worry. Just do a "gut check." Take out your mobile phone, and browse your website. Is it likely that a customer coming FROM Google on their mobile phone and landing ON your website will convert, meaning purchase your product on an e-Commerce site, or fill out a registration form on a site that wants sales leads? If so, leave your mobile turned "on" in AdWords. If not, turn it off.

To adjust your bids on mobile, click into a Campaign (as these settings are Campaign-specific). Next, click Devices in the left column and you should see the Device targeting box appear. Having decided whether to decrease (or increase) your bids on mobile devices, select a positive or negative number in the Bid adj. (bid adjustment) column. If mobile is outperforming desktops and tablets, you can up your bid. It just depends on what's performing.

Here's a screenshot:

	Level: **Campaign**; Conversions > **0.00**			
☐	Device	Level	Added to	Bid adj.
☐	Mobile phones	Campaign	JM - Bay Area	-100%
☐	Computers	Campaign	JM - Bay Area	— ☑
☐	Tablets	Campaign	JM - Bay Area	— ☑
	Total: Account			

Do this, if, and only if, you believe (or know for a fact) that mobile traffic isn't converting for you. In some rare situations, the reverse may occur: desktop traffic does not convert, but the mobile does. In that case, then turn off or bid down the desktop by setting a bid adjustment of -100% or some lesser percentage. The point is that you need to pro-actively decide which devices to run your ads on, not let Google think for you.

⟩⟩⟩ DELIVERABLE: AN ADWORDS GOTCHA CHECKUP

Now that we've come to the end of Chapter 1, it's time for your **DELIVERABLE**, a completed *AdWords Gotcha* worksheet. This worksheet will query you as to the four "Gotchas" to make sure that you have pro-actively decided on your AdWords strategy as opposed to being led by the nose by Google against your own best interests.

For the **worksheet**, go to **https://www.jm-seo.org/workbooks** (click on "AdWords Workbook 2018," enter the code 'adwords18' to register if you have not already done so), and click on the link to the "AdWords Gotcha" worksheet.

3

KEYWORDS

When a user goes to the Google search engine, he or she inputs a keyword search query such as "motorcycle insurance" or "pizza near me." Because **keywords** drive Google in a fundamental way, you, as an advertiser, must be very strategic and very systematic in how you use keywords to trigger your ads. Choose the *wrong* keywords, and you'll waste money. Choose the *right* keywords, and you're on your way to making money. Choose the *right* keywords, block *irrelevant* queries via negative keywords and proper match types, and create *tight* Ad Groups that structurally reflect your keywords, and you'll be on your way to making a *lot* of money via AdWords. This Chapter is a deep dive into the art and science of choosing keywords.

Let's get started!

TODO LIST:

» Learn Some Keyword Theory

» Brainstorm Your Keywords

» Reverse Engineer Competitors' Keywords

» Use Google Tricks to Identify Possible Keywords

» Use the SERPS.com Keyword Tool

» Master Google's AdWords Keyword Planner

»» Deliverable: A Completed Keyword Brainstorm Worksheet

» Identify Your Main Keyword Structural Patterns

» Create Your Keyword Worksheet

»» Deliverable: Keyword Worksheet

Not all keywords are created equally! Let's take our hypothetical "cat grooming salon" here in San Francisco, "Jason's Cat Grooming and Cat Boarding Emporium, Inc." or "Jason's Cat Emporium" for short.

Cats only! No dogs allowed!

As a business, therefore, we are targeting San Francisco residents who have cats, who have money, and are interested in either our grooming services or our cat boarding services (or both). Remember that we also have an online store that sells cat toys and paraphernalia to customers across the USA.

We thus have three distinct product or service offerings:

1. **Cat boarding services** – boarding cats for San Franciscans who need a place for fluffy to stay while the vacation at Cabo, or travel to New York City.
2. **Cat grooming services** – providing hair styling to cats in San Francisco so that they look their best
3. **Cat toys and paraphernalia** – an online e-Commerce offering of the very best in cat toys and products.

We suspect that our customers go to Google and type in search queries such as:

cat boarding

pet boarding

cat grooming

kitty boarding

kitty grooming

feline boarding

feline grooming

cat toys

cat collars

hypoallergenic cat litter

etc.

Now, as a potential Google AdWords advertiser, we need to know a little about **keyword theory**. We want to advertise to our best customer segment (rich people geographically located in San Francisco who have cats that they need to be groomed and/or boarded as well cat lovers across the USA who are looking for unusual and high quality cat toys) and avoid our worst customer segments (poor or cheap people who can't afford quality cat boarding or grooming services, or (even worse) people looking for dog grooming, dog boarding, or exotic bird services). Our high-end cat toys target folks who love their cats possibly as much, or more than, their spouses and children and for whom money is no object.

AdWords is a Game of Words

You want to think of AdWords as a "keyword game" among you, Google, and your competitors to identify the most profitable keywords and eliminate money-losing keywords. It's all about focus and strategy. Take a moment to review the theoretical constructs below. These will help orient your mind to see that a "word" is not "just a word" when it comes to AdWords.

Educational Search Query. This is a keyword query when a person is just starting out to learn something about something. Examples would be "Siamese Cats," "Where to buy a cat," or "How to Cut a Cat's Claws."

Transactional Search Query. This is a keyword query when a person isn't really in "learn mode" but rather is in "purchase" or "buy mode." (Practitioners often call these "buy keywords" or "late stage keywords."). Examples would be "Cat Boarding," "Cat Boarding in San Francisco," or even "Pet Boarding." "Cat grooming" or "cat grooming service" would also be transactional keywords, albeit focused on the less valuable grooming service vs. the more profitable boarding service. Ditto for "cat collars" or "personalized cat collars."

Micro Search Query. This means a unique search query, such as "Cat Microchipping," "Luxury cat boarding," or perhaps "Iguana Boarding." "Diamond cat collar" would also fit as a micro. These queries are just a few words, but so specific as to be a very precise search term.

Short- or **Long-Tail Search Query**. This is not my favorite way to conceptualize search queries, but basically, a "short tail" is just a few words vs. a "long tail" which is more than a few words. A short tail would thus be "cat boarding," and a long tail would be "cheap cat boarding in the Castro District, San Francisco." Here's a tip: focus less on the number of words, and more on the user intent, be that educational or transactional.

Branded Search Query. Your company name, as in "Jason's Cat Emporium" or "JM Internet Group." Your **competitors' names** are also branded search terms (and can be good to advertise on if you're brave).

Reputational Search Query. This is when a user is seeking to research your "reputation" and usually appends the word "review" to your company name as in "Jason's Cat Emporium Reviews."

Negative Keyword. This is a keyword that is definitely NOT your customer. For example, if someone types in "cheap cat boarding" you might consider the word "cheap" as a *negative* keyword, as it indicates the person has no money or is very budget conscious. "Free" is a common negative keyword as it indicates a person who is not willing to pay.

Ambiguous Keyword. This is a keyword that could be your target customer but might include some folks who are decidedly not your customer. "Pet boarding" or "Animal boarding" would be examples, as these might include both "dog people" and "cat people."

Transactions Are Where It's At

In general, as you build out your Keyword Worksheet you're looking for **transactional keywords** that are definitely your customer vs. educational keywords that might indicate a person with no money or no desire to spend. Be sensitive as well to **ambiguous** keywords that could be your customers AND some non-customers, and watch out for negative keywords like "cheap" or "free" that indicate poor people or people with no intention of spending money.

FOCUS ON TRANSACTIONAL KEYWORDS

Another way to think about keywords is to group them into "hot" keywords that are a) definitely your customers, and b) definitely ready to buy vs. "warm" or "cold" keywords that are a) probably not your customers, or a mix of desirable customers and non-desirable others, and/or b) persons in a frame of mind that are not quite ready to buy.

Volume vs. Value

Keyword **volume** has to do with how many search queries hit Google in a given time period; for example, a month. You can get this data from the *AdWords Keyword Planner* inside of AdWords, under the *Tools* menu (marked with a Wrench icon, top right of the screen).

Value has to do with the estimated cost-per-click of the keyword. I like to think of volume and value using the analogy of "fish in a pond."

> **Keyword** = type of fish. Is it a salmon or a tilapia? A carp or a bass? Is it *cat boarding* or *cat grooming* or *cat collars*?
>
> **Volume** = number of fish in the pond. There may be 1000 tilapia in the pond, but only 100 salmon. There may be thousands of (low value) searches for *cat collars* and just a few for *luxury cat boarding San Francisco*.
>
> **Value** = the price per pound in the fish market, or what people are willing to pay. Even if you know nothing about fish, the fact that organic salmon is $19.99 a pound and farmed tilapia is just $2.00 a pound is a strong clue that the former is "yummy" and the latter "not so much." The fact that the cost per click in AdWords for *cat boarding* is more than for *cat collar* is a signal that the former has more money behind it than the latter.

You can derive this data from the *Keyword Planner* (inside AdWords under Tools) and the SERPS.com *keyword research database* (**http://jmlinks.com/24z**). Check out the complete list of keywords tools via the dashboard at **http://jmlinks.com/dashadwords**.

VIDEO. Watch a video on how to use the Google AdWords Keyword planner (Old Interface) at **http://jmlinks.com/25a**. **Note**: be aware that must have a paid AdWords account with some dollar spend for the tool to give detailed data! You can watch a separate video at **http://jmlinks.com/25b** that overviews alternative keyword discovery tools.

Riches are in the Niches

Generally speaking, you are looking for "high volume," "high value" keywords that are transactional. So, if you board cats, groom cats, and sell cat stuff, you are looking to advertise on

cat boarding – YES! Definitely your customer. Plus variations like "luxury cat boarding" or "cat boarding in San Francisco" or "Castro District cat boarding," etc.

pet boarding – Maybe! This is an ambiguous keyword (it could be dog people, after all).

cheap cat boarding – probably not, as a person who enters this into Google is indicating he has little or no money.

free cat boarding – definitely not, as a person who enters this into Google is indicating he has little or no money.

animal boarding – Maybe! This is an ambiguous keyword (it could be dog people, after all).

kitty boarding – Yes!

cat grooming – Yes!

feline boarding – Yes!

kitty grooming – Yes!

overnight cat boarding – definitely!

quality cat boarding – definitely!

dog boarding – No!

personalized cat collars – Yes!

diamond cat collars online – Yes!

personalized diamond studded cat collars money is no object – Yes, Yes!

If you were to board iguanas or exotic birds, then *iguana boarding* or *exotic bird boarding* would be excellent "riches in the niches" types of keyword queries.

>> BRAINSTORM YOUR KEYWORDS

With a little keyword theory under your belt, it's time to being to brainstorm your keywords in a systematic way. Sit down in a quiet place with a good cup of coffee or tea, or if you prefer, a martini, i.e., *anything to get your ideas flowing*! Brainstorm the **keywords** that a customer might type into Google that are relevant to your company, your product, and/or your service.

Ask yourself:

When a potential customer sits down at Google, what words do they type in?

Which keywords are DEFINITELY those of your customers?

Which keywords are CLOSE to a decision to buy? Which are farther away, earlier in the sales ladder?

Which customer segments use which keywords, and how might keywords differ among your customer segments?

Which keywords match which product or service lines as produced by your company?

Which keywords or helper words are definitely NOT your customers? Free or cheap, for example, are often markers of people who have little to no money, or no inclination to spend.

Be sure to capture your synonyms – lawyer vs. attorney, boarding vs. hotel, cat vs. kitten as well as your more ambiguous umbrella terms like law firm or pet boarding.

Conduct a Keyword Brainstorming Session

I highly recommend that you organize a formal keyword brainstorming session with your marketing team (it might be just you by yourself, or it might be your CEO, your marketing manager, and a few folks from the sales staff). Devote at least ONE HOUR to brainstorming keywords; close the door, turn off the cell phone, tell your secretary to "hold all calls" and start drinking (either coffee or martinis).

Brainstorm, brainstorm, brainstorm the keywords that customers are typing into Google. Try not to miss any possible keyword combinations!

Do this, first, individually – take out a piece of paper, and write keyword ideas down WITHOUT talking to the others in your group.

Don't be shy. Don't leave anything out. The goal is to get EVERYTHING on paper, no matter how ridiculous it might be.

Then have a group session and go over all the keywords each person has identified.

Drink some more coffee, or more martinis, and keep brainstorming – write all possible keywords on a whiteboard, a piece of paper, or a Word / Google document.

Don't censor yourself because there are no wrong answers. The goal of this exercise is to get the complete "universe" of all possible keywords that customers might type into Google.

BRAINSTORM ALL POSSIBLE TARGET KEYWORDS

For your first **TODO**, open up the "keyword brainstorm worksheet" in either Word or PDF, and begin to fill it out as completely as possible. For the worksheet, go to

https://www.jm-seo.org/workbooks (click on "AdWords Workbook 2018," and enter the code 'adwords18' to register if you have not already done so), and click on the link to the "keyword brainstorm worksheet."

Again, for right now, don't worry about the *organization* of your keywords. Don't police your thoughts. Write down every word that comes to mind - synonyms, competitor names, misspellings, alternative word orders. Let your mind wander. This is the keyword discovery phase, so don't exclude anything!

» REVERSE ENGINEER COMPETITORS

After you've completed this first wave of brainstorming, let's you and your group members do some searches on Google for target keywords. Take a few of the keywords you've already identified, and type them into Google. As you search Google, identify your "Google competitors," that is, companies that are on page one of the Google results and therefore doing well in terms of SEO (Search Engine Optimization). Even though this Workbook focuses on AdWords, you can use the organic results to **reverse engineer** their keywords for *SEO* and use these as possible keywords for *AdWords*.

Here's how.

Method #1: Source Code

First, click over to their homepage or whatever page is showing up on page one of Google for a search that matters to you. Next, view the HTML source code of this page. To do this, in Firefox and Chrome, use *right click*, then **V**iew, **P**age Source. In Internet Explorer, use **V**iew, **S**ource on the file menu. Finally, find the following tags in the HTML source code:

```
<Title>
<Meta Name="Description" Content="...">
<Meta Name="Keywords" Content="...">
```

If you have trouble finding these HTML tags, use CTRL+F (on a PC vs. Command+F on a Mac) on your keyboard, and in the dialog box type *<title, description,* or *keywords*

For each, write down those keywords your competitor has identified that might also be applicable to you. Here's a screenshot of

http://www.globalindustrial.com/c/hvac/fans, one of the top Google performers for the search "industrial fans" with the three critical tags circled -

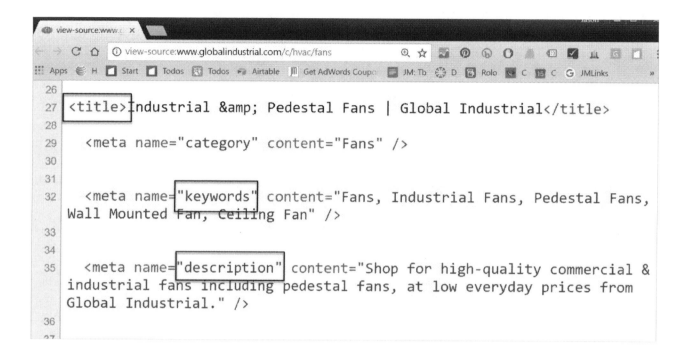

(**Note**: you may not find all of these tags in competitor pages, and don't worry about what they actually do as those are questions of search engine optimization. Just use them as ways to look into the minds of competitors for keyword ideas).

Read each tag out loud to your group members. Notice how each tag in the source reveals the "thought process" behind this page, showing the "types" of fans people might search for - pedestal, wall mounted, ceiling, etc. The goal of viewing the source of your competitors' pages is to "steal" their keyword ideas and write down any relevant keywords onto your "keyword brainstorm" document.

> **VIDEO.** Watch a quick video tutorial on how to use "view source" to reverse engineer competitors at **http://jmlinks.com/5k**.

Method #2: Ads on AdWords

Do searches that you have already brainstormed, and read the ads out loud that you see on the Google screen. Here, for example, are ads returned from the search "San Francisco Cat Boarding:"

San Francisco Cat Hotel - Large suites, all day play & love
`Ad` www.thepawington.com/ ▼
Plus Free SFO Airport Parking 24/7!
Highlights: Luxury Experience, Friendly Resort, Grooming And Spa Services...
Grooming · Daycare · Reservations · Boarding

SF Premier Pet Boarding - Try Us, Tour Us, Love Us - 24/7/365
`Ad` www.waghotels.com/ ▼ (888) 924-5463
First time offers call 888-WAG-LINE
San Francisco · Make A Reservation · Services · Faq's · Contact Us · About Us
📍 25 14th St, San Francisco, CA - Open today · Open 24 hours ▼

Rover.com - Cat Boarding - Find Cat Lovers Near You
`Ad` www.rover.com/Cats ▼
4.9 ★★★★★ rating for rover.com
In-Home Trusted 5-Star **Pet Boarding**
Get Stay Photos · 24/7 Emergency Support · Avg. Price $15 - $40 · In-Home Dog Sitting
Sleep soundly with premium insurance and photo updates – Today.com
Premium Insurance · Sit A Dog, Save A Life · Free Rover Mobile App · Search Sitters · Jobs At Rover

Kitty Charm School - Private Bedrooms, Loads of Love
`Ad` www.kittycharmschool.com/ ▼
Rooms Start at just $27. NO CAGES

As you read this out loud, you'll see synonyms (e.g., *cat* vs. *kitty* vs. *pet*) and helper words such as *premier, private, hotel, boarding,* and points of difference such as "large suites" or "private". Write these down on your list. For example, notice how the first ad has a headline of "Cat Hotel." Bingo! You've found a new word, *hotel* as in *cat hotel.* Be sure to click over to the companies who are advertising, and View Source looking at their TITLE, META DESCRIPTION, and KEYWORD tags.

Use Keyword Spying Tools

As you research your keywords, you can avail yourself of free / paid tools that "spy" on competitors. One of the best is SpyFu at **https://spyfu.com/,** and another is Keyword Spy at **http://www.keywordspy.com/.** I am partial to Keyword Spy because if you sign up for just a free account, they give you a lot of information on competitors. Simply enter a keyword and see who's advertising, what their ads say, and some research on their keyword targets.

By entering *thepawington.com* into Keyword Spy, for example, I learn that they are advertising on:

> *San Francisco pet hotel*
>
> *San Francisco dog hotel*
>
> *Pet hotel San Francisco*
>
> *Pet grooming*
>
> *Cat resorts*

By doing this, I get some great synonyms to "cat boarding" such as "cat hotel" or "cat resort." Who knew?

For your second **TODO**, open up your "keyword brainstorm worksheet," and jot down the top five competitors who appear at the top of Google for your target keywords, use the tactics above to view their source, and then write down keyword ideas taken from their TITLE, META DESCRIPTION, and META KEYWORDS tags. Be sure to input them into Keyword Spy or SpyFu as well.

Did you discover any keywords you left out in your first brainstorming session? If so, be sure to write those on your list.

» USE GOOGLE TRICKS TO IDENTIFY POSSIBLE KEYWORDS

After you have brainstormed keywords and used View Source to view the keywords of competitors, it's time to use free Google tools for keyword discovery. Here are my favorite strategies starting with Google's own free tools.

First, simply go to Google and start typing your keyword. Pay attention to the pull-down menu that automatically appears. This is called **Google Suggest** or **Autocomplete** and is based on actual user queries. It's a quick and easy way to find "helper" words for any given search phrase. You can also place a space (hit your space bar) after your target keyword and then go through the alphabet typing "a", "b", etc.

Here's a screenshot of **Google Suggest** using the key phrase "motorcycle insurance":

Hit your space key after the last letter of the last keyword (e.g., after *motorcycle insurance*) and more keyword suggestions appear. You can also type the letters of the alphabet – a, b, c, etc. and Google will give you suggestions. Here's a screenshot for the letter "b":

Google

motorcycle insurance b

motorcycle insurance b**roker**
motorcycle insurance b**rackets**
motorcycle insurance b**est**
motorcycle insurance b**log**
motorcycle insurance b**y state**
motorcycle insurance b**y the month**
motorcycle insurance b**ased on cc**
motorcycle insurance b**asics**
motorcycle insurance b**est rates**
motorcycle insurance b**efore or after buying**

Google Search   I'm Feeling Lucky

Report inappropriate predictions

Second, type in one of your target keyword phrases and scroll to the bottom of the Google search page. Google will often give you **related searches** based on what people often search on after their original search. Here's a screenshot for "motorcycle insurance" -

Searches related to motorcycle insurance

cheap motorcycle insurance   **how much is** motorcycle insurance

cheapest motorcycle insurance   motorcycle insurance **comparison**

motorcycle insurance **rates**   motorcycle insurance **cost**

best motorcycle insurance   **average** motorcycle insurance

Note the **helper words** it tells you people use to search: cheap, rates, best, "how much," comparison, cost, and average. Are these not wonderful clues as to how customers search Google? As you look at Google autocomplete and related searches, add these keywords to your master list.

SEO Chat's Autocomplete Tool

A third party tool that pulls data from search queries is SEO Chat's tool at **http://jmlinks.com/25y**. Simply enter your core keyword phrase such as "cat boarding" or "industrial fans," and this tool polls Google, Bing, YouTube, and Amazon for related phrases. Here's a screenshot:

Another good tool is Keywordtool.io at **http://jmlinks.com/25z**. It basically types through the alphabet for you and gives you nifty keywords. Spend some quality time with the Google tools as well as these two suggestion tools, using your "starter" keywords and looking for synonyms and helper words.

VIDEO. Watch a quick video tutorial on how to use Google autocomplete and related searches to generate keyword ideas at **http://jmlinks.com/18n**.

For your third **TODO**, open up your "keyword brainstorm worksheet" and write down some keyword ideas garnered from these free tools. You want a messy, broad and complete list of the "universe" of possible customer keywords via your own brainstorming process, via reverse engineering your competitors, and now via Google and third-party keyword tools. The objective is to get everything down on paper.

≫ USE THE SERPS.COM KEYWORD TOOL

With your rather messy list of keywords in hand, it's time to start focusing on **volume** vs. **value**. Unfortunately, the best tool (which is Google's *AdWords Keyword Planner*) does not provide complete keyword data to new accounts or accounts with little spend. So I recommend that you check out the SERPS.com tool at **http://jmlinks.com/29g**. Enter one of your foundational or "core keywords" such as *cat boarding*, or *cat grooming* into this tool. Click "I'm not a robot" to do the captcha, and hit search.

This tool then gives you *keyword* ideas (left column), *volume* (second column) and *CPC* or value (third column). *Ignore the value column as it isn't very helpful*; just use CPC as a good proxy for the value.

Here's a screenshot for *knee surgery*:

Keyword Search Results

Keyword	▼Volume	CPC	Value
filter keyword			
knee surgery	12,100	$4.07	$49,247.00
arthroscopic knee surgery	8,100	$4.62	$37,422.00
knee surgery recovery	1,600	$1.64	$2,624.00
knee surgery game	1,000	$1.56	$1,560.00

You can see that knee surgery has a volume of 12,100 searchers per month, and a CPC of $4.07, meaning advertisers are willing to pay Google approximately $4.07 for a click. Now, enter a few terms that correspond to the educational vs. transactional queries and compare volumes and values. Here's a summary:

Keyword	Volume	CPC
knee surgery	12,100	$4.07
back of knee pain	6,600	$1.13
causes of knee pain	1,600	$1.60
knee surgeon	480	$3.34
best knee replacement surgeon	110	$5.21

As you work with this tool, pay attention to:

Core keywords. These are the foundational keywords such as *knee pain, knee surgery, knee surgeon* as well as *orthopedic surgeon*. Similarly, you could see that you have *cat boarding* vs. *cat grooming* vs. *cat toys* for the Cat Emporium example. "Which fish do you want to catch?," so to speak.

Volume. More is generally better, as you want to advertise on terms that have sufficient volume to indicate that real people are searching. "Fish where the fish are," so to speak.

Value as Measured by CPC. Ignore the Value column in the tool, and pay attention to the CPC or Cost Per Click column. Generally, the higher the CPC, the more money is behind the search. In the example above, you can see that *back of knee pain* is worth only $1.13 vs. *best knee replacement surgeon* is worth $5.21, indicating which one is most likely to have a lot of money behind it. "Catch yummy fish," so to speak.

As you input your terms into this tool, your goal is to start seeing keywords as groups as in the group around "knee surgeon" vs. "orthopedic surgeon" and to look for which groups have the highest volume and highest values. There is a tradeoff of course. The higher the volumes, generally the lower the value. You're looking for the sweet spot of relatively high volume with relatively high value.

Finally, be on the lookout for "secret fishing holes." These are keywords that may not show high CPCs, but they still get you good customers. For example, a knee surgeon might specialize in *arthroscopic knee surgery*, for example, or in *knee surgery for athletes*. If you can find focused, niche keyword that yield lots of customers but your competitors haven't bid up the AdWords cost-per-click, you've found a "secret fishing hole."

» MASTER THE GOOGLE ADWORDS KEYWORD PLANNER

Now it's time to use the most comprehensive keyword tool of them all: Google's own official **AdWords Keyword Planner.** It's free, but you'll need an AdWords account to use it fully.

VIDEO. Watch two quick video tutorials on how to use the Google AdWords Keyword Planner *in general* at **http://jmlinks.com/17j** and *to brainstorm keywords* at **http://jmlinks.com/18m**.

Sign up for AdWords

To sign up for AdWords, go to **http://adwords.google.com/**. You'll need a credit card to set up an account, and the Google interface will attempt to get you to start advertising right away.

AdWords will FORCE you to set up your first campaign, with groups, ads, and keywords. Simply follow their instructions "as if" you were going to set up an ad, and immediately set your first campaign to "pause." To pause your campaign, follow the AdWords set-up instructions to set up your account and then click on the "campaigns" tab, select the checkbox to the left of your first campaign, click "edit" in the menu, and then "pause." (You can even call AdWords at 866-246-6453 and ask them for help on how to set up your advertising campaigns, and then *sneakily* ask them to **pause your campaigns** – just explain that you are just setting things up, right now, and you do not want to turn on any advertising at this time). The point of all this is to use a credit card to set up an active AdWords account, and then use this account to access the Keyword Planner.

Note: do NOT let the "helpful" Google employees "help" you set up your AdWords Campaigns, as they will run wild and you'll overspend. We want to be much more focused and selective than the Googlers would lead us to be.

Google Goes Evil

Google now requires that you spend money to get accurate data out of the Keyword Planner. Sadly, Google as a monopoly is acting as a monopoly and refusing to provide accurate keyword data to those who do not have established AdWords accounts spending money. In my opinion, this is a violation of the public trust the Google has a near monopoly on search, but absent government regulation, it's Google's world – we just live in it! This also creates problems if you are just starting out, in that you won't have as much data to work with as an established advertiser.

Accordingly, you may need to allocate a few hundred dollars and run some actual ads before you'll get accurate keyword information out of the tool. I know it's a bit of a pain, but once you have an operational AdWords account, you can use the Google AdWords Keyword Planner as a wonderful way to research keywords. Let's return to the Keyword Planner.

Use the AdWords Keyword Planner Tool to Identify Keywords

Now that you're signed in to your AdWords account, next, go to the "Tools" tab at the top underneath the "Wrench" icon, and scroll down to "Keyword Planner." Here's a screenshot:

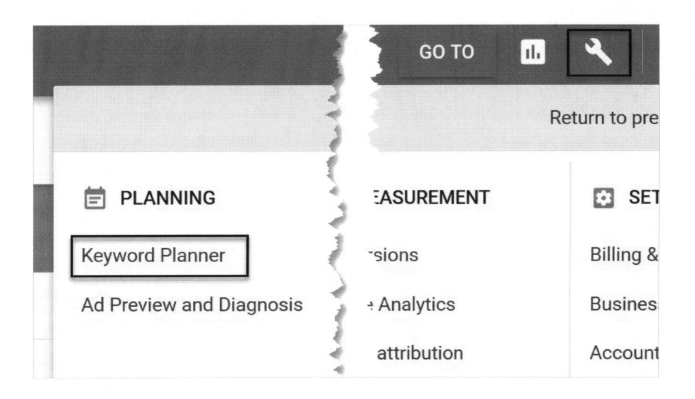

Here's how to use it.

First, get past the "welcome screen" by typing your keywords underneath "Search for new keywords using a phrase, website or category" and hitting the blue "Get Ideas" button. This will get you into the actual tool. Here's a screenshot:

This gets you into the tool's real interface. This is where you'll do most of your work, and it looks like this:

A Poor User Interface

A note to the wise. The Keyword Planner is not going to go down in Google history as the best-designed user interface! To be blunt, Google has done a pretty terrible job with the user interface, but because of Google's search dominance, it remains the data source for keyword research. Google has the data, and you have to master the Keyword Planner! Just be patient, and click around on the tool to learn its operation and secrets.

For purposes of our example, let's assume we are a New York orthopedic surgeon specializing in knee surgery, and so we'll enter "knee pain." After you click "get ideas," you'll see a tab called "Ad group ideas," and one called "keyword ideas." Scroll down under the "ad group" ideas and click "into" the various suggested groups. Google will give you good ideas for related keywords here.

For instance, if you type in "knee surgeons," Google will give you these suggestions:

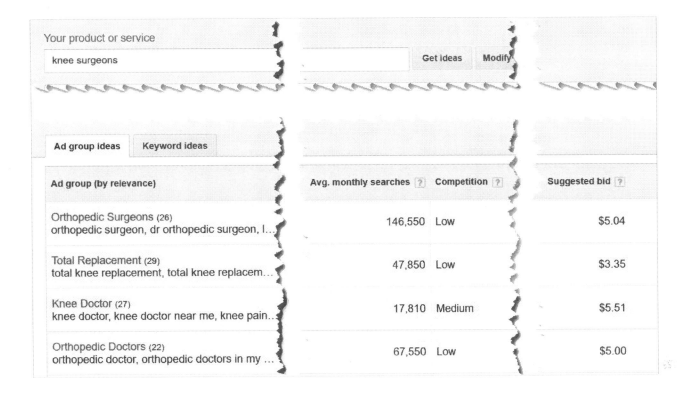

So Google is grouping relevant keywords around *Orthopedic Surgeons* at 146,650 searches per month, *Total Replacements* at 47,850 searches per month, *Knee Doctor* at 17,810 and finally *Orthopedic Doctors* at 67,550. Note also the suggested bids which, more or less, reflect the average cost-per-click you'll pay if you advertise on those keywords. Google is indicating that the more transactional searches like *Knee Doctor* come in at $5.51 per click, vs. the more educational searches like *Total Replacement* at $3.35. Click into an Ad Group Idea, and you can drill down into more ideas.

Click on any group, and Google will drill down into more related searches. All of these give you great ideas for possible keywords. Note that it also gives you Avg. monthly searches (volume) and suggested bid (value) information; a rough approximation for how frequently a keyword phrase is actually used.

Play around with the tool and look at the Ad Group ideas to brainstorm all possible core keywords that matter to your company, as you start to organize your keywords into tight groups centered around one keyword.

Don't Miss Your Synonyms!

Returning to *knee surgeons*, notice how the tool gives you both *helper* words and *synonyms*. Click on the Keyword Ideas tab, and you get a drill down into various search terms. Similar to the Serps.com tool, you get a column of ideas, one of volume, and one of value – indicated by AdWords as "Keyword (by relevance), "Avg. monthly searches" (volume) and "Suggested big" (value). Here's a screenshot:

Keyword (by relevance)	Avg. monthly searches [?]	Competition [?]	Suggested bid [?]
orthopedic surgeon	135,000	Low	$5.07
knee replacement	60,500	Medium	$3.52
knee surgery	22,200	Medium	$4.00
orthopedic doctor	60,500	Low	$5.21
total knee replacement	22,200	Medium	$4.09
knee replacement surgery	22,200	Medium	$3.66

If you don't see these columns, click on the Columns tab to enable. them. Here's a screenshot:

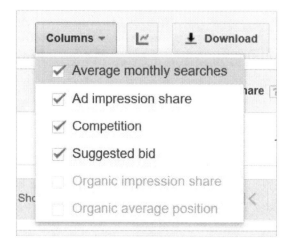

As you browse through keywords, look for both helpers and synonyms or adjacent keyword groups. For example,

> *knee surgery* = a person considering knee surgery. Don't miss knee surgeon as this is the highly transactional search for the person.

> *orthopedic surgeon* = a different core keyword for a different group. Note how this is a higher level of generality as there are hip, shoulder, knee, etc. specialists within orthopedic surgeons.

Also, pay attention to helper words. For example, you get *best* knee replacement, telling you that *best* is a helper word, and you get *doctor* as well as *surgeon, orthopedic* as well as *knee*. The tool is telling you how people search: some people search for *knee doctors*, and others for *orthopedic surgeons*. Many people search for *best* knee surgeons (and to the contrary, few search for *worst* knee surgeons). Because to Google, *a word is just a word*, you want to be sure to capture ALL your key synonyms. A search for "best knee doctor in San Francisco" is different from a search for "best orthopedic surgeon in San Francisco," even though the latter may include the former, i.e., many people searching for orthopedic surgeons who do knees. This is true across all domains; a *lawyer*, to Google, is not the same as an *attorney*. In summary be sure to identify all your helpers and synonyms, and write these down on your Keyword Brainstorm Worksheet.

The Left Column

Next, you'll want to play around with the tool and understand some of its more advanced features. Let's start with the columns and pull-outs mean. Starting on the left column, take a look at "Targeting." You'll see here it will default to "All locations" or perhaps "United States." If you click the pencil to the right of "United States," you can drill down to specific states or even cities by typing their names into this space and then clicking "remove" on other entries. This is useful if you'd like to know keyword search volume for specific states; at the city level, the tool isn't very useful as the search volume is often insufficient, however. Alternatively, you can "remove" the United States and target "All locations" which is "Google speak" for the entire world.

Generally speaking, you'll need a broad geography: so choose "United States" rather than "Tulsa, Oklahoma" to research "industrial fans," "cat boarding," or "knee surgeons" as you brainstorm keywords. If a search is too narrow, the tool returns zero data. Zero data does not mean that there is no volume; the tool is just a bit bizarre, and at low volumes just gives up. That's Google for you.

The **Negative keywords** feature also has some utility. You can filter "out" keywords that don't matter to you. For example, if we type in "exercises" it then filters out keyword phrases that contain the word "exercises." Many companies want to filter out words like "free" or "cheap," so use negative keywords for any desired refinement.

Refocusing the Keyword Planner

You may notice that the tool gives you very broad and often irrelevant keyword suggestions, so I often recommend that you refocus it to just your target phrase and related phrases. To do this, on the left-hand column where it says "Keyword Options," click there, and then select "Only show ideas closely related to my search terms" by moving the blue button to "on" and clicking on the blue "save" button. Here's a screenshot:

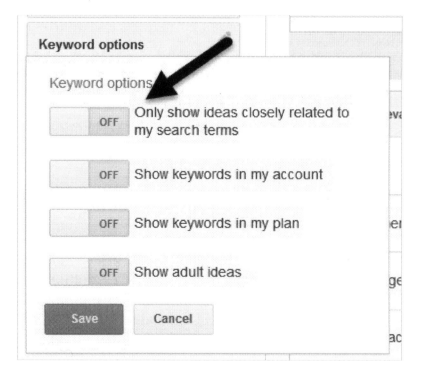

Once you click "off" to "on" for "Only show ideas closely related to my search terms," you've reset the Keyword Planner to zero in on more specific keywords. Once you've done that, you should see something like this:

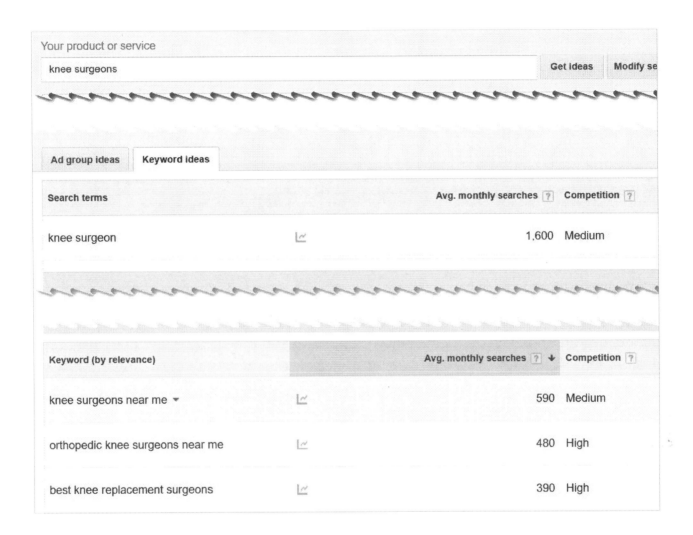

Now click on the column "Avg. monthly searches," and the tool will sort your keywords by volume (the number of searches per month for your target geography). The above screenshot is for "knee surgeons" after having focused the tool by entering "knee surgeons" with location set to "United States," and "Keyword filters" set to "Only show ideas closely related to my search terms":

You can see the average monthly search volume for "knee surgeon" is 1,600. The number 1 phrase is "knee surgeons near me" at 590 followed by "orthopedic knee surgeons near me" at 480. **Note that these search volumes refer to exact match** only: they take into account only when a searcher enters that phrase and nothing more.

For example, phrases like "knee surgeons in Tulsa," or "best knee surgeon" are not included in the 1,600 volume total. It is for exactly *knee surgeon* and nothing more, and nothing less. There is no easy way to get a phrase volume out of the tool, sadly.

(**Note**: the volumes you see may differ from the above, or you may see a "range" of volumes if you have not spent enough money in AdWords. Take all the volumes in the tool as illustrations only – despite Google's public brand persona, the tool seems to be incredibly inaccurate! Use it more to get a sense of range, which keywords are more popular than others as opposed to a scientific treatise on actual keyword volumes).

If you'd like to drill down to a phrase, then you have to re-enter it in the top. Enter "back of knee pain," and Google will give you the related helper words such as "pain behind knee cap," "sharp pain behind knee, etc."

Comparing Phrases

Unfortunately, the Keyword Planner gives only "exact match" data, so you have to manually enter a bunch of related keyword phrases and then tally them up to get a total for phrases. You can, however, enter multiple phrases and compare them. Let's set our location to New York, NY, and let's take these keywords:

> *knee pain*
> *knee surgery*
> *knee surgeon*
> *knee surgeons New York*

To compare phrases, enter them as a <u>comma-separated phrase</u> as follows and click "Get ideas":

> *knee pain, knee surgery, knee surgeon, knee surgeons New York*

In this way, you can compare search terms head-to-head, looking at keywords, volume, competition, and value. Here's a screenshot:

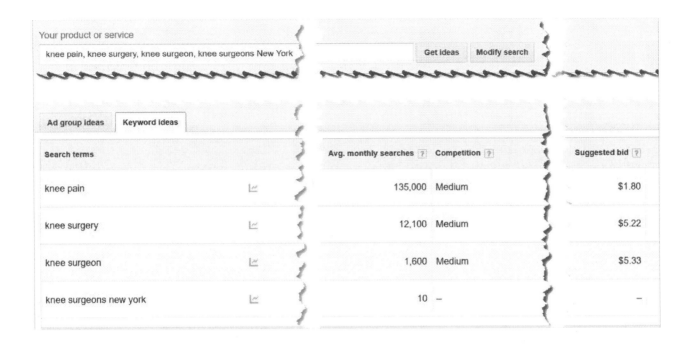

Keyword Volume vs. Value

To understand what this all means, let's return to our analogy of **fishing** and **fish**. As the AdWords technician, you're the **fisherman** of course.

First, you want to "fish where the fish are." This is telling you that there's a lot of volume for *knee pain*, medium volume for *knee surgery / knee surgeon*, and just a little for *knee surgeons New York*. So *knee pain* has lots of volume at 135,000 but little value at only $1.80 CPC vs. *knee surgeon* at 1,600 and $5.22 and probably the best term *knee surgery* at 12,100 and $5.22.

In short, the AdWords marketplace is telling you that "knee surgeon" and "knee surgery" are worth MORE than "knee pain" even though "they have far less volume.

Why? Well, think about what each search query tells you about the customer need.

> *A search for "knee pain" might be someone who needs an aspirin (a $1.00 sale at best), while a search for "knee surgeon" is probably someone who is looking for surgery (easily $50,000).*

"Knee pain" is an "educational" search by someone who is using Google to learn vs. "knee surgeon," which is a "transactional" search by someone who is using Google to find a surgeon to buy knee surgery from.

In general, "educational" searches will have lower average costs-per-click indicating lesser value that "transactional" searches; AdWords is giving you strong clues as to "where the fish are," and "which fish are yummy to eat."

Your competitors using AdWords, in short, are bidding up the keywords that are likely to end in sales and thus telling you which keywords are valuable for your own AdWords efforts!

UNDERSTAND THE VOLUME / VALUE TRADE-OFF

More on Educational vs. Transactional Keywords

Another way to look at this is that keywords that are *early* in the sales ladder usually occur when a person is just learning, just educating himself about an issue and not likely to buy something. Remember, these are called **educational keywords** and generally have low cost-per-click in AdWords. Keywords that occur *late* in the sales ladder are when they are looking to buy something, or make an engagement. These are called **transactional keywords** and generally, have high cost-per-click in AdWords. In general, you want to optimize for transactional keywords if possible.

VIDEO. Watch a quick video tutorial on distinguishing educational vs. transactional keywords, volume vs. value at **http://jmlinks.com/18k**.

Your **best AdWords advertising** occurs at focused, transactional keywords, not educational keywords. You're looking for the "sweet spot" between volume and value, educational and transactional.

Let me emphasize this:

Identify and advertise on transactional, late stage, high-value keywords.

A knee surgeon wants to advertise on Google for "San Francisco Knee Surgeons" and not for "knee pain," because the former are potential patients looking for knee surgery, and the latter could be practically anyone with a sore knee and just needing an aspirin.

Don't Believe Everything Google Tells You

Note here that if you call into AdWords Tech Support, they will often advise you to "go broad" and advertise on high volume, early stage, educational search terms. Don't do it! Similarly, inside AdWords, you will sometimes get "suggested keywords" via the AdWords interface. Either you'll be prompted inside of AdWords, or you can click on the **"Opportunities"** tab in AdWords to see these autosuggestions. Click on the blue Keywords & Targeting button, and AdWords will often suggest a cornucopia of keywords that generally have high volume (i.e., are educational) and not transactional in nature. For example, here's a screenshot from an Ad Group focused on *accountant* (the transactional search focused on hiring a person / accountant):

Notice how Google wants me to add *accounting* (an incredibly broad and vague term), as well as *business accounting* – both as broad match. That is, no quotes, no bracket, and no plus sign – a sure fire way to dramatically increase clicks and costs, but not necessarily conversions. So use the "Opportunities" tab just as a first step in brainstorming keyword ideas if you are already advertising, not as an endpoint. It tends to suggest very broad, educational, high volume keywords that will wreck your focus.

Don't fall for Google's so-called opportunities!

That said, you still need to rely on your instinct to determine your best keywords and then bolster that with real data from your Google Analytics, which we discuss in Chapter 7. The Keyword Planner is only a tool, and the art of AdWords still means a lot of head-scratching to identify those keywords that are not just high volume but also high value.

Riches are in the Niches

Back to fishing, if you want to "fish where the fish are" (*high volume keywords*) and "catchy yummy fish" (*high-value keywords*), you also want to find "secret fishing holes." These are keyword phrases that tend to yield good customers, <u>yet your competitors have not discovered</u>. They are less expensive in AdWords and easier to optimize for via SEO (because they are undiscovered). If you discover a "secret fishing hole" vs. one everyone knows about, you have struck gold (to mix metaphors). Don't tell anyone! **Riches**, in sum, are in the **niches** when it comes to keywords and AdWords.

For "knee pain," the niche search is "knee surgeon" or better yet, "best knee surgeons in the Bay Area."

Here's another example. Let's assume you sell *auto insurance*. The generic "auto insurance" keyword query will have a lot of volume, and a lot of value, and be pretty difficult to show up high on Google AdWords without paying a bundle because of intense competition. In this case, look for "niche" keywords such as "auto insurance for teens," or "auto insurance for high-risk drivers," or even "auto insurance for classic cars." You may find that highly profitable niches of your business reflect highly profitable keyword queries for your AdWords advertising, and – to the extent that your competitors are ignorant – a "secret" niche keyword is the best of all.

Get ALL Your Keyword Ideas Down on Paper

For your next **TODO**, open up your "keyword brainstorm worksheet," and jot down keyword volumes and the CPC values of relevant keywords. Again, don't worry about being organized. Just indicate – in general – which keywords are higher volume vs. higher value, which ones are educational vs. transactional. It won't be a perfect map, but you will start to see patterns as to volume and value.

▸▸ DELIVERABLE: A COMPLETED KEYWORD BRAINSTORM WORKSHEET

Now we've come to the end of this process, and you should have the first Chapter **DELIVERABLE** ready: your completed **keyword brainstorm worksheet**.

Remember the "Keyword Brainstorm" document will be messy. Its purpose is to get all relevant keywords, helper words, and keyword ideas about volume and value down on paper. In the next step, we will turn to **organizing** our keywords into a structured **keyword worksheet**. This will be our blueprint for setting up our AdWords campaigns and groups.

▸ IDENTIFY YOUR MAIN KEYWORD STRUCTURAL PATTERNS

After you complete your **keyword brainstorm** worksheet, your head may be spinning (*especially if you and your team were using martinis rather than coffee as the drink of choice during the brainstorming exercise*). Now it's time to shift gears and to organize those keywords into "structural patterns" with an eye to both keyword volume and value.

Here's where we're going:

> **Brainstorm** *your keywords >* **organize** *them into a keyword worksheet >* **organize** *your AdWords account into* **keyword-centric Ad Groups**.

Let's look at some example websites.

Most businesses have a few different product or service lines, and often a few different customer segments. Take a look at Progressive Insurance (**https://www.progressive.com/**), for example, and you'll quickly realize that they have different types of insurance offered such as auto insurance, motorcycle insurance, RV insurance, and even Segway insurance. Take a look at **https://www.progressive.com/insurance-choices/** to see the organizational structure of their website, and you'll quickly realize that the "structure" of the website reflects the "structure" of how people search for insurance. Those who are on a Harley-Davidson motorcycle are searching in one way, and those looking to insure their Segway are searching in another.

So in terms of **keyword structural patterns** and **match Ad Groups** (and website landing pages), we have:

motorcycle insurance =

> a group of keywords around *motorcycle insurance* like *cheap motorcycle insurance, motorcycle insurance quote*, etc. =
>
> an Ad Group in AdWords =
>
> a landing page on the website.

Car insurance =

> a group of keywords around *car insurance* like *cheap car insurance, automobile insurance, car insurance quote*, etc. =
>
> an Ad Group in AdWords =
>
> a landing page on the website.

etc.

Or, take a look at Industrial Fans Direct (**http://www.industrialfansdirect.com/**), and you'll see that they have product categories such as blowers, man coolers, ceiling, bathroom fans, etc., and that these reflect the "needs" of consumers who "search Google" using words that reflect those needs.

blowers =

> a group of keywords around *blowers* =
>
> an Ad Group in AdWords =

a landing page on the website.

roof exhaust =

a group of keywords around *roof exhaust* =

an Ad Group in AdWords =

landing page on the website.

etc.

With those examples in mind, it's time to look at your own keyword patterns.

Take a look at your own **keyword brainstorm document**, and circle the "core keywords" that reflect your basic product or service categories. Usually, you'll see a one-to-one correspondence of a "product group" that matches a "core keyword," as you see in the examples above. And you'll also see a bunch of helper words like *cheap, best, San Francisco, quote, rate*, etc., that are often entered alongside the core keyword. People often mistakenly think that they have "hundreds" of keywords, when in fact they usually have only about five to ten **core keyword groups** or **structural patterns**, and these then form hundreds of possible keyword queries. As on *Progressive.com* and *IndustrialFans.com* as listed above, you'll see that a core keyword should become one, and only one, landing page on the website.

In terms of AdWords, this means:

One *core keyword* will (ultimately) become one *group* in AdWords account.

To return to Jason's Cat Emporium, we'd have:

A *cat boarding* Ad Group

A *cat grooming* Ad Group

A *cat toys* Ad Group

Looking to the future, however, if *luxury cat boarding* generates a really strong ROI, then we'd break out luxury cat boarding into its own unique Ad Group. We'd also have an Ad Group for *pet boarding*, recognizing that this is an ambiguous pattern vs. *cat boarding*. AdWords **strongly rewards** a **tight match** between a *core keyword*, a corresponding *Ad Group*, corresponding *keyword triggers, corresponding ads* that contain the keyword in visible ad text, and a corresponding unique *landing page* on your website. Your keyword worksheet should group your target keywords into this structure.

> **VIDEO.** Watch an official Google video on how to organize your AdWords account by keyword-based groups visit **http://jmlinks.com/39n**.

Keyword Volume and Value

As for keyword *volume* and *value*, you'll then see that you take a core keyword and you can look at the volume of the entire "group" of keywords around it, as well as the value as measured in Google's Keyword Planner that reflects the "value" of these keywords in the sense that they are likely, or not, to end in a sale.

> **Volume** = are there a lot, or just a few, searches on Google that reflect the core keyword?
>
> **Value** = if a searcher enters this search query is it of high, or low value, to your company, as measured in the likelihood that it can become a sale, and if it becomes a sale that that sale makes you a lot (or just a little) of money?

For your next **TODO**, download the **keyword worksheet**. For the worksheet, go to **https://www.jm-seo.org/workbooks** (click on 'AdWords Workbook 2018,' and enter the code 'adwords18' to register if you have not already done so), and click on the link to the "keyword worksheet." Note this is a Microsoft Excel document.

VIDEO. Watch a video tutorial on how to create a Keyword Worksheet at **http://jmlinks.com/17m**. Note: this video is focused on SEO, but many of the same rules apply to AdWords.

Inside the document, list each major pattern of your keywords (which reflect a product or service grouping of your company) on a line all by itself in the first column. Return to the Google AdWords Keyword Planner and note both the keyword volume and keyword value (suggested bid) that correspond to each core keyword.

>> CREATE YOUR KEYWORD WORKSHEET

Now it's time to fill out your keyword worksheet in more detail. In your spreadsheet, you'll be filling out columns for the following:

> **Core Keywords**. These are the minimum words necessary to create a relevant search. If you are a watch repair shop servicing high-end watches, for example, your core keywords would be phrases such as "watch repair," "Tag Heuer Repair," "Rolex Repair," etc. This is the first column, and reflects the core, structural keyword patterns and indicates volume and value.
>
> > **Note.** If, to your business, a phrase is important enough (e.g., *Rolex watch repair* vs. *Tag Heuer watch repair* vs. just *watch repair*), then break it out into its own core keyword group / line item on your keyword worksheet. Do this even if these words are closely related (e.g., Rolex repair vs. Hamilton repair vs. Tag Heuer repair for watches).
>
> **Helper Keywords**. Common helpers are geographics like San Francisco, Berkeley, and Oakland. In the watch examples above, other helpers would be "best," "authorized," "NYC" etc. that combine with the core keywords to make the actual search query (e.g., "Best watch repair NYC").
>
> **Sample Search Query Phrases**. Take your core keywords plus your helpers and build out some "real" search queries that potential customers might use. Group these by keyword family. For example, you'd have a keyword group called "Rolex Repair" and underneath, related keyword phrases such as "Rolex Repair NYC," "Authorized Rolex Repair Midtown," or "Best Rolex Repair Shop New York," etc.

Search Volumes. Indicate the volume of searches (where available) as obtained from the Google AdWords Keyword Planner.

Search Value. Indicate whether a given keyword family is of high, low, or negative value to you and your business. Does it indicate a searcher who is probably a target customer? If your answer is strongly yes, then this is a "high value" search term! Does it clearly indicate a non-customer? If so, this is a "low value" or even a "negative" search term. I often mark "hot," "warm," or "cold" next to a keyword group.

Competitors. As you do your searches, write down the URL's of competitors that you see come up in your Google searches. These will be useful as mentors that you can emulate as you build out your SEO strategy.

Negative Keywords. Are there any keywords that indicate someone is definitely not your customer? Common examples are *cheap* or *free*, as these are often indicative of people with little or no money, or little or no intention to buy something. *(These negative keywords are not so important for SEO, but for AdWords, it is CRITICAL to brainstorm your negative keywords.)*

Priority Order

Not all keywords are created equally. Some are **high volume** (*lots of searches*), and some are **high value** (*they are customers ready to buy something, or take an important action like filling out a feedback form, or calling with an inquiry*). With respect to your business, take a look at your keyword worksheet and think about which queries are a) the *most likely* to be a potential sale, b) the *most likely* to be a high-value sale, and c) the *least likely* to be ambiguous. (An ambiguous or problematic keyword is one that has several meanings, that might cross business products or services, and is, therefore, more difficult to optimize on than an unambiguous keyword. Compare *fan* for example, which could be a *hand fan*, an enthusiast for a *sports team*, or an *electrical appliance* to *blow air* with *insurance* which refers to one, and only one, type of product. *Pet boarding* or *animal boarding*, for example, are ambiguous vs. *cat boarding* or *dog boarding*.)

VIDEO. Watch a video tutorial on educational vs. transactional, volume vs. value keyword theory at **http://jmlinks.com/17n**.

Prioritize Your Keywords: Hot, Warm, or Cold?

Prioritize your keyword families on the spreadsheet from TOP to BOTTOM with the highest priority keywords at the top, and the lowest at the bottom.

Remember the *volume* vs. *value* trade-off. "Transactional" keywords (those close to a sale) tend to have higher *value*, but lower *volume*; "whereas educational" keywords (those early in the research process) tend to have lower *value*, but higher *volume*.

However, here's the rub: because of the see-saw between value and volume, there is no hard and fast rule as to what should be your top priority. It can't be just *volume*, and it can't just be *value*.

In fact, I recommend you use a column on the far left and call it "hot / warm / cold." Sit down with the CEO or sales staff, and play a "hot / warm / cold" game by asking IF a customer entered such-and-such into Google, would it be hot (*definitely our customer*), warm (*probably our customer*), or cold (*not our customer*)?

Prioritize the "hot" keywords at the top of the Keyword Worksheet, and the "warm" keywords towards the bottom. I often throw out the "cold" keywords entirely. This will help you see the complexity of keyword patterns as some keywords will be "easy" to see as hot / warm / cold, and others might be more challenging – perhaps they have a lot of volume, but are ambiguous, or perhaps they are high value but just so little volume, or the customers don't know to search for them.

> *The art of AdWords is targeting the keywords most likely to generate high ROI, which is a function of BOTH volume and value as well as whether a keyword is unambiguously your customer or ambiguously your customer plus others.*

The Art of AdWords

Don't stress your keyword organization too much!

Your keyword worksheet is a *living* document. As you build out your AdWords campaigns and groups and measure your rank and results, you will "tune" your advertising to work on those keywords that are high value, high volume, and you can actually out-compete the competition for. It's a process, not a static result. Online advertising, like cooking great food or preparing for a marathon, is as much *art* as *science*. Don't fall prey to **analysis paralysis**, and endlessly analyze your keywords as opposed to implementing them.

The basic concept to get is:

Keyword Group = AdWord Group in AdWords

So you identify core keywords that will be at the center of unique AdWords Groups. For example:

Cat boarding = one AdWords Group

Cat grooming = one AdWords Group

Cat Toys = one AdWords Group

In summary, the **keyword worksheet** for your company should reflect keyword *volume, value* (as measured by the "fit" between the keyword search and what your company has to offer), and the *structural search patterns* that reflect the "mindset" by which people search. These will become your AdWords ad groups.

▶▶ DELIVERABLE: YOUR KEYWORD WORKSHEET

After some brainstorming, hard work, and organization, you should have your **DELIVERABLE** ready: a completed **keyword worksheet** in an Excel or Google spreadsheet. The first "dashboard" tab should be a high-level overview to relevant keywords, reflecting the structural search patterns that generate the **keyword groups**, next the keyword volumes as measured by the Google keyword tool, and finally the values measured by the Google cost-per-click data and your own judgment as to which search queries are most likely to lead to a sale or sales lead. Other tabs (which you will fill out over time) include a tab for reporting, a tab to measure your rank on Google vs. keywords, a tab for local search rank, and a tab for landing pages.

> **Note**: *I recommend one Keyword Worksheet for both your SEO project and your AdWords project. If for now, you are only working on AdWords, it may be more Spartan, but – long term – you want to think of both SEO and AdWords as working together for an effective Google strategy. Ditto for Bing / Yahoo.*

Your keyword worksheet is your blueprint for successful AdWords, but don't think of it as a static document! Rather, think of your keyword worksheet as an evolving "work in progress."

4

SEARCH NETWORK

When people say they want to "advertise on Google," they generally mean that when a customer searches on Google for *such-and-such* product, service or company by keyword, they want their ad to appear on the Google search engine, and nowhere else. As we've learned so far, however, Google is actually two distinct networks (*Search* and *Display*), and if you're not careful, Google can place your ads on the Display Network as well as the Search Network without your pro-active understanding. In this Chapter, we'll exclusively focus on tips, tricks, and best practices for the **Google Search Network** so as to show your ads when (*and only when*) you want them to appear on Google and its Search Partners like Yelp or Comcast.

Let's get started!

TODO LIST:

>> Review Basic Set Up Best Practices

>> Identify Transactional Keywords

>> Organize Your Campaigns & Ad Groups

>> Use Correct Keyword Match Types

>> Write "Attract / Repel" Ad Copy

>> Use Ad Extensions

>> Follow CEA on Landing Pages

>> Set Your Bids

>> Set Logical Campaign Settings

>> Choose Your Geotarget Settings Wisely

>> Monitor Your Bids and Performance

>> Shoot Your Dogs, and Let Your Winners Run

>> Learn about a Special Type of Search Ad: Google Shopping Campaigns

>> >> Deliverable: Search Network Worksheet

>> REVIEW BASIC SET UP BEST PRACTICES

We'll assume you've set (or reset) at least one Campaign to run *exclusively* on the Search Network. Here are the steps to create a new Campaign:

1. Log in to your AdWords account.
2. Click on *Campaigns* on the left.
3. Click the White "+" sign in the blue circle.
4. Select "Search Network Only."
5. Make sure that the "Include Display Network" box is NOT checked (i.e., you are running ONLY on the Search Network.)
   a. You can include *Google search partners* if you like. Or if you are on a tight budget, uncheck this.
6. Follow the steps to set up an at least one Ad Group that matches one of your Core Keywords, at least one ad inside that Ad Group going to a matching landing page on your website, and keywords (as indicated below) using "+", """, or "[]" around your target keywords. (*We'll return to this, in detail, later in this Chapter*).

And here are the steps if you have an existing Campaign. Click into the Campaign, and then click on the *Settings* tab and then *Networks*. Where it says *Type*, change it until you see "Search Network only – All Features." Here's a screenshot:

Here's a (not-so) fun fact. Nowhere does Google publicly identify the companies in the Search Network. We know it's Yelp and Comcast, for example, but there isn't a clear list of all sites in the Search Network, nor does AdWords identify where your ads appear if you leave the box checked. So, if you're cynical, I'd uncheck this box to be sure your ads run only on Google.com. That's the safest thing to do, so I usually uncheck "Search partners."

Say No to the Display Network (For Now)

If you see "Display Network" anywhere, you've done something wrong. Sometimes if you've set up a Campaign running on the "Display Network," AdWords will not let you convert it to the "Search Network." In that case, you have to pause that Campaign and create a new one in the correct fashion. At the end of this process, you want at least one Campaign that is set to run on *only* the Search Network. In fact, you never want to "mix networks." You should have campaigns running only on the Search Network and if you decided to use the Display Network, another set of campaigns running only on the Display Network. Mixing the networks in one Campaign complicates everything, so **don't mix campaigns**.

> **VIDEO.** Watch a video from Google on the Google Search Network at **http://jmlinks.com/26d**.

▶▶ IDENTIFY TRANSACTIONAL KEYWORDS

Let's revisit your keywords and explain how to input them into your Search Campaign > Ad Groups. Keywords drive search, and – therefore – *keywords* drive AdWords on the Search Network. Here are the steps from the perspective of a customer

Customer need > search query on Google > click on ad > landing > sale / sales inquiry

Or, translated into our scenario of a San Francisco resident who needs cat boarding for Fluffy, during his vacation to Cabo San Lucas:

I need to have my cat taken care of on vacation > keyword search on Google for "cat boarding San Francisco" > see / click on ad for Jason's Cat Emporium > land on Jason's website > fill out inquiry form to check out the Emporium for my cat, Fluffy > Agree to sign up Fluffy, and the deal is done.

Using this simple process model, you can see that your steps on AdWords begin with defining the best **keywords** to advertise on.

Step #1: Identify the search keywords that you want to advertise on.

It all starts with the keyword. The customer need "becomes" the keyword, and the keyword that the customer enters into Google needs to find a match in the keyword that you enter as a **keyword trigger** into AdWords.

Customers enter **keywords** into Google.

Advertisers enter **keyword triggers** into AdWords.

While Google calls both of these *keywords*, it's helpful to distinguish between the *keywords* that are entered by the searcher, and the *keyword triggers* that you, as an advertiser, enter into AdWords. Keyword triggers as we shall see, need to be notated in AdWords in one or more of three distinct ways:

Plus Signs

+cat +boarding = telling Google to run your ad on any variations of the words *cat* and *boarding*, but no substitutions.

Quotation Marks

"cat boarding" = any keyword query by the searcher that includes that phrase.

Brackets

[cat boarding] = the exact phrase, only, as entered into Google.

No Plus Signs No Quotes No Brackets

The "sucker choice" is to enter in the words *cat boarding* into AdWords with no "+" sign, no "quotation," and no "[" bracket.

NEVER JUST ENTER KEYWORDS INTO ADWORDS!

The reason, of course, is that if you just enter

cat boarding

Google can substitute nearly *anything* for those words, and before you know it, you're running on

dog hotels

Because to Google, the word *cat* is like the word *dog*, and the word *boarding* is like *hotel*. Entering keywords with no quotes, plus signs, or brackets is a "gotcha," so don't do it!

Core Keywords

Refer back to Chapter 3, and your Keyword Worksheet. You should have identified **core keywords** that reflect the major structural patterns of your products or services. Take a look at the Progressive.com website (**https://www.progressive.com/**), and you'll see a very structured organization of keywords in terms of landing pages on the website.

*Auto / car insurance at **https://www.progressive.com/auto/***

*Home insurance at **https://www.progressive.com/homeowners/***

*RV insurance at **https://www.progressive.com/rv/***

*Motorcycle insurance at **https://www.progressive.com/motorcycle/***

*Boat insurance at **https://www.progressive.com/boat/***

etc.

In addition, as you look at their landing pages and read the text out loud, you'll notice helper keywords such as *quote, rates,* or *companies* that further make a keyword transactional. In fact, here's a screenshot of their ad running on "motorcycle insurance":

Progressive® Motorcycle - Progressive.com

Ad www.progressive.com/Motorcycle ▼

Get an instant quote today from America's #1 **motorcycle** insurer!

Get A Quote · Norton Secured Site

Ratings: Selection 9.5/10 - Ease of purchase 9/10 - Website 8.5/10 - Service 8.5/10

And here's their ad for "boat insurance:"

Boat Insurance Rates - See How Much Progressive® Can Save You

Ad www.progressive.com/Boat ▼

Get A Free Quote & Buy Now!

You'll see that Progressive runs very specific ads for "boat insurance" that go to a very specific landing page for "boat insurance" vs. very specific ads for "motorcycle insurance" that go to a very specific landing page for "motorcycle insurance" and so on and so forth.

Check it out yourself. Do some searches relating to *car insurance, RV insurance, boat insurance*, etc., and click on the ads. Notice how many of the top advertisers send you to very defined landing pages even if they offer other products or services.

AdWords rewards a **very organized, hierarchical structure**, as follows:

> One core keyword > one specific Ad Group > one or more specific ads > one specific landing page

Identify Transactional Keywords

On your own Keyword Worksheet, you should have identified 5-10 **core keywords** plus another 10-20 helper words that ensure that your keywords are **transactional** in nature. You also want to keep an eye on keyword **volume** and **value** because, since AdWords is expensive, you generally want to advertise only on keywords that are likely to lead to a sale. In general, (but not always), *educational* keywords should be avoided.

A San Francisco orthopedic surgeon, for example, might have core keywords such as:

Knee surgery

Knee surgeon

Hip surgery

Hip surgeon

Shoulder surgeon

Shoulder surgery

Orthopedic Surgeon

And helper words like *San Francisco, best, top, top-rated, arthroscopic, second opinion,* etc. (He will NOT advertise on "knee pain" as that "educational keyword" will have a lot of volume, generate a lot of clicks, cost him a lot of money, but end up with many bounces as these are people who are not close to the decision to engage with a knee surgeon). Also, let's say he only focuses on knees. Then he might run ads only on the "knee surgeon" pattern and avoid the more general "orthopedic surgeon" as this will pull in people looking for hip or shoulder surgeons.

In general, the tighter your focus among your keyword target, your Ad Group (and ads), and your landing page, the better you'll do on AdWords.

Similarly, for Jason's Cat Emporium, we will identify transactional keywords such as:

cat boarding

cat hotels

long-term cat care

cat kennels

cat grooming

cat toys

And avoid educational / non relevant keywords such as:

cat

cat vets

dog boarding

And realize that some relevant keywords are problematic (because they may signify other animals such as dogs):

pet boarding

animal boarding

And some helper keywords are negative (poor or cheap people)

cheap

free

To review what we learned in our Keywords Chapter, your first **TODO** is to build out your **keyword worksheet**, organize your keywords into core keywords, and identify transactional keywords that are also (hopefully) high volume / high value. I would also create a column, and designate the core keywords as "hot" (definitely your customer), "warm" (probably your customer), "cold" (probably not your customer). It's also a good idea to notate keywords like *pet boarding* that are **problematic** because they include both your customers and non-customers. (We'll return to ambiguous keywords when we discuss writing ads in the "Attract / Repel" style).

Generally speaking, **one** core keyword should be represented in **one** ad group in AdWords. Where we're going is to see that your Keyword Worksheet will map to your AdWords as follows:

one core keyword > one Ad Group in AdWords

for example:

cat boarding > cat boarding group in AdWords

pet boarding > pet boarding group in AdWords

cat hotel > cat hotel group in AdWords

cat kennel > cat kennel group in AdWords

cat grooming > cat grooming group in AdWords

DON'T LET REALITY CONFUSE YOU

While you might think that *pet boarding* includes *cat boarding* (which it does in the real world), at the "word game" level of AdWords, you want a very tight focus between the words. Don't be lazy and clutter your Ad Groups with non-related keywords. So *pet boarding* will get its own Ad Group, *cat boarding* will get its own Ad Group, and so on and so forth.

The tighter the linkages, the better your performance will be.

Campaigns in AdWords

But before we dive deeper into strategy and setup, let's talk for a moment about **Campaigns** in AdWords

Conceptually, a campaign should reflect a budgetary "bucket" of how you want to spend some money in a strategic fashion. They should reflect customer segments as well. Since campaigns are where you set the *network* (Search vs. Display), plus features such as *geotargeting* and *device targeting*, you want to think strategically about your campaigns as you get started (or revise existing campaigns).

As examples:

Networks. Since "search" is radically different from "browse," the MOST important campaign setting is to ONLY run a campaign on ONE network, the Search Network (not *Search Network and Display Network*) (*despite what Google tells you is the "best choice!"*).

Geotarget. "Geotarget" or "location targeting" is AdWords lingo for showing ads ONLY to people who reside in a specific area (e.g., San Francisco) and/or are searching with intent around that area (e.g., "Cat Hotels San Francisco") vs. showing your ads just to anyone, anywhere. Location targeting is set at the campaign level; accordingly, if you want to show different ads to people in different cities, then you set this at the Campaign level, and you need separate campaigns (e.g., one for San Francisco and one for Oakland).

Budget. If you make a lot more money on one product (e.g., *cat boarding*) than on another (*cat grooming*), it makes sense to put them in separate campaigns as budgets can be set separately at the Campaign level.

Devices. Since you can determine whether you show on mobile phones vs. desktops vs. tablets by changing these settings at the campaign level, and budgets are set at the campaign level, it makes sense to split your mobile from your desktop campaigns if (for some reason) you want a different spend for people searching on different devices.

Ad Groups

Next, once you've set up a campaign, drill down into your **Ad Groups**. Remember:

one core keyword = one ad group in AdWords

Also, remember that even though you can geotarget in AdWords, city names are also often helper keywords, so you'd have *cat boarding San Francisco* in the *cat boarding* Ad Group. Finally, although structurally in AdWords Ad Groups "live" inside of Campaigns, AdWords will force you to set up a group and an ad the first time when you set up a Campaign, so you often have to toggle back and forth as you set things up.

ADWORDS IS A HIERARCHY

Structurally, however, AdWords works as a **hierarchical system**:

Account (sets account information, access, controls billing, etc.)

Campaign (sets budget, geotarget, devices, etc.)

Ad Group (organized around ONE and ONLY ONE core keyword) controls ads and bids and contains the keywords.

Here's a nice graphic from Google that displays the hierarchy of AdWords:

Account			
Unique email and password Billing information			
Campaign		Campaign	
Budget Settings		Budget Settings	
Ad Group	Ad Group	Ad Group	Ad Group
Ads Keywords	Ads Keywords	Ads Keywords	Ads Keywords

Source: **http://jmlinks.com/39v**.

For example, I'd have a Campaign called **Cat Emporium – Search Network** that is running on the Search Network only, geotargeting residents of San Francisco. Here's a screenshot showing the hierarchy of *Campaign > Ad Group* from inside an account:

In the AdWords New Experience, the Campaign is off to the far left in the menu system but also appears at the top in the "breadcrumb" trail as I have indicated above. Also note how I have four ad groups, one for *cat boarding*, one for *cat hotels*, one for *cat kennels*, and one for *pet boarding* that reflect the core keywords of *cat boarding, cat hotels, cat kennels*, and *pet boarding*. I usually name my Campaigns with their network, making it easy to see what's what at a glance. So by naming the Campaign *Cat Emporium – Search Network*, I can see in an instant that this is a Search Network campaign.

While you can zig and zag through AdWords, up and down the levels, it is immensely helpful always to ask yourself "what level am I at?"

Account

Campaign

Ad Group

Ads ("live" at the Ad Group level)

Keywords ("live" at the Ad Group level)

You can "view" items like keywords across levels, like looking into a glass building that has different floors but you can only edit / change them when you are actually "at" a specific level. With respect to keywords, for example, you can "view" them across Campaigns, but you can only edit / change them at the Ad Group level. A few things, such as bids, can be set at two levels (e.g., you can change a bid at the Ad Group level or at the Keyword sublevel).

Since *cat grooming* is quite different from *cat boarding*, then I'd have a separate campaign called *Cat Grooming*, with at least one Ad Group in it, also called *Cat Grooming*. And, to advertise my cat collars, cat toys, and other cat paraphernalia via Google Shopping ads (an XML feed from my e-Commerce store), I'd also have a Campaign called e-Commerce with groups for the main product groupings. Since e-Commerce is nationwide and very different from the boarding and grooming functions, I'd set up a unique Campaign for that.

VIDEO. Watch a video tutorial from Google on setting up Ad Groups at **http://jmlinks.com/26b**.

» USE CORRECT KEYWORD MATCH TYPES

Next, you need to properly understand and use AdWords nomenclature to set your keyword targets. Google confuses this by misleading you into thinking you can just throw keywords into AdWords willy-nilly.

Keyword Match Types

Taking our example of *cat boarding*, in your Cat Boarding Ad Group, you'd insert the keyword:

+cat +boarding

meaning, *modified broad match* in AdWords speak.

which tells Google to run your ad if, and only if, the searcher enters BOTH the word *cat* AND the word *boarding* (as well as very close variants such as the plural *cats*, or a misspelling like *baording*). I also recommend you enter variants such as

"cat boarding"

meaning, "phrase match" in AdWords speak

and

[cat boarding]

meaning, "exact match" in AdWords speak

And you would **NEVER** enter just

cat boarding

as this is the **dangerous broad match** in AdWords. If you enter just *cat boarding* (no "+" plus sign, no """ quotation marks, no "[" brackets, as Google will run away with this, and run your ads on things like *pet boarding, dog boarding, iguana boarding, dog hotels*, etc.

Here's a screenshot of keywords correctly entered into AdWords:

		Keyword ↑	Status	Max. CPC
☐	●	+cat +boarding	Eligible	$2.01 (enhanced)
☐	●	+luxury +cat +boarding	Eligible	$5.01 (enhanced)
☐	●	[cat boarding]	Eligible	$2.01 (enhanced)
☐	●	"cat boarding"	Eligible	$2.01 (enhanced)

Enter All Three Variants

Why enter

> "cat boarding"
>
> [cat boarding]

when

> +cat +boarding

is the superset of the former two keyword phrases, meaning it **includes** them by default?

> Technically speaking, you do not have to enter all three variants because +*cat* +*boarding* captures the other two.

However, if you also enter the phrase and exact match variants, you get better reporting (you'll know exactly how many searches occur for the *exact keyword query, the phrase, and then variations of the phrase*), plus you can **set your bids differently** for these keywords. (*I've also noticed that entering all variants seems to help your performance... don't ask me why just do it*).

You can use the AdWords Wrapper tool at **https://jmlinks.com/25c** to quickly create all variants this. Just be sure to enter your core keywords and select **ONLY** the "+Modified +Board, 'Phrase' & [Exact] Match" box. Here's a screenshot:

```
+Modified +Broad, "Phrase" & [Exact] Match

  +cat +boarding
  "cat boarding"
  [cat boarding]




3 Lines                              Copy
```

You can then copy / paste those into the Keywords tab / Ad Group level for the corresponding Ad Group in your AdWords Campaign.

High-Value Keyword Phrases

Similarly, for more targeted bidding, if a phrase might have higher value to you, you can enter it as a phrase. For example:

same day cat grooming

luxury cat grooming

in-home cat grooming

The reason for this is that the addition of certain helper words indicates that the customer is more likely to be affluent, and/or willing to pay a premium.

Accordingly, you want the option to be able to raise your bid for these variations of your keyword. Indeed, if a phrase is really, really valuable (e.g., *same day cat grooming*), you can even break it out into its own Ad Group for specialized management! Howie Jacobson (*AdWords for Dummies*, 2007) likens this to a "special trailer" on a Hollywood movie set for a superstar.

> **TODO.** Consider breaking out high-value phrases into their own keyword phrases for special bidding or reporting, or even creating a specific Ad Group for each high-value phrase.

Google's Official Explanation

Despite the official Google help explanation (**http://jmlinks.com/23d**), using broad match (just the words, without quotation marks, plus signs, or brackets) can produce many poor matches. If you just enter

cat boarding

as a keyword trigger into AdWords (no plus sign, no quotes, no bracket), Google will substitute words: *cat* will become *pet*, *boarding* will become *vet*, and your ad will be running on *pet vets* before you know it! Google doesn't easily explain this (*for nefarious reasons?*), but you can see what keywords you're actually running on by going into an Ad Group, clicking on the Keywords tab, and then clicking on Search Terms. Here's a screenshot showing terms generated from the phrase "dental implants" (or +dental +implant):

SEARCH KEYWORDS	NEGATIVE KEYWORDS	SEARCH TERMS ▼

☐	Search term	Match type	Added/Excluded
	Total: Search terms		
☐	all on 4 dental implants	Phrase match	None
☐	full mouth dental implants	Exact match	✓ Added
☐	same day dental implants	Exact match	✓ Added
☐	full dental implants cost	Phrase match (close variant)	None
☐	dental implants price	Broad match	None
☐	cost of full dental implants	Phrase match (close variant)	None

You want to do this for any and all *Ad Groups > Keywords* on an on-going basis, looking for really good, high converting keywords (which you then break out into their own special Ad Group) and really bad, low converting keywords (which you abandon or even add as negative keywords).

Stay Organized. One Keyword Group = One Ad Group

Do NOT jumble keywords into ad groups willy-nilly! For example, if you have a keyword group for *cat grooming* do NOT put keywords relating to *cat boarding* into that group. The same goes for closely related but distinct keywords:

cat kennel

cat boarding

cat hotel

In the real world, these are the SAME THING, but in AdWords these are DIFFERENT, and each should have its own UNIQUE Ad Group. That's the best practice, but if you're pressed for time (*or just lazy*), you can put very closely related keywords into the same group. You might put all three in one Ad Group (again, *if you're lazy*), but that's not the best practice (*because you want specific ads to show for each keyword, which we'll discuss in a minute*).

> *Like a well-organized dresser, Google wants the socks in the sock drawer, the underwear in the underwear drawer, and the pajamas in the PJ drawer. Even better they want the red socks in the red socks drawer, the blue socks in the blue socks drawer, etc. Don't mix things up!*
>
> *Hey, and don't call my Mom and tell her just how disorganized my own "real world" dresser drawers are; at least my AdWords Campaigns > Ad Groups are organized, Mom!*

AdWords is a Word Game

Also, realize that AdWords is a word game; do not put the keyword phrase *pet grooming* in a mangled Ad Group either. To AdWords, "pet" is a different word than "cat," so – accordingly – it should have its own Ad Group, meaning:

cat boarding = its own Ad Group

pet boarding = its own Ad Group

animal boarding = its own Ad Group

If there is a very close synonym (such as *animal* for *pet*), it is probably OK to include both of those keyword phrases in one group. So you might have:

pet / animal group = keywords that are derivations of *pet boarding* and *animal boarding*.

That said, it is **always** better to split and have highly focused Ad Groups than to combine (related) keywords into one Ad Group. I would split *pet* and *animal* into different Ad Groups.

> *AdWords rewards tight, highly focused Ad Groups over unfocused keyword groups!*

Also at a conceptual level, realize that some keywords are unambiguously your customers (e.g., *cat boarding*) and others may or may not be your customers (*pet boarding*); this is a major reason NOT to mix keywords of the one into the Ad Group of the other. It's also a reason to separate them by Campaigns, so you can always run full blast on your tight Campaigns (*cat boarding* / definitely our customers) vs. your ambiguous Campaigns (*pet boarding* / maybe not our customers).

In summary, the tighter more organized the matching between the keyword group and the ad group, the better you will be in the long run.

> **AdWords rewards very tight, very focused Ad Groups, organized around very tight, very focused keywords!**

Keyword Insertion

AdWords has a feature called **Keyword Insertion**, formerly called *Dynamic Keyword Insertion*. In this technique, you write your ads using a snippet of code. For example, you'd write an ad headline like:

> *Buy {Keyword Chocolate}*

and enter keyword triggers like

> *"Dark Chocolate Bar"*
>
> *"Sugar-Free Chocolate"*

"Gourmet Chocolate Truffles"

(Remember to use plus signs, quotation marks, or brackets! And note that in this methodology the capitalization does matter).

Next, if the keyword trigger / keyword query is short enough to fit into your headline, then AdWords automatically replaces *Chocolate* with the keyword query entered by the user. So if they enter *dark chocolate bar* on Google, your ad headline would not say *Buy Chocolate* but rather *Buy Dark Chocolate Bar*

In this way, the ad appears, to the user, to be laser-focused on what he or she just entered. If you have hundreds or thousands of closely related keywords, Keyword Insertion is a time-saving option in AdWords. (You can read the full Google help file at **http://jmlinks.com/26v**).

I would use caution when deploying Keyword Insertion, however, because, in my experience, it tends to hurt the Quality Score vs. ads that are manually written with a tight focus between the keyword trigger and the actual keyword in the ad headline / text. In addition, Keyword Insertion can allow you to be lazy and jumble up your Ad Groups to Keywords, even though a disorganized Ad Group > Keyword relationship will hurt your ad performance in the long run.

So use Keyword Insertion with caution. I'd recommend it only for large companies, with thousands of keyword patterns, and especially for very focused e-Commerce Campaigns. Google even has a feature called *Dynamic Search Ads* in which Google will automatically pull your website content or an XML feed of your product data and write your ads on the fly. (Read about it at **http://jmlinks.com/26w**). Again, I would be very cautious about letting Google do all the hard-thinking for me.

Negative Keywords

Negative keywords are "stop" words that tell Google NOT to run your ad if they are entered. *Cheap* is a common negative keyword or stop word. So if you enter *cheap* as a negative word (at either the campaign or group levels), then any time someone enters *cheap*, your ad will NOT show.

> **VIDEO.** Watch a video from Google on how to use negative keywords in AdWords at **http://jmlinks.com/26m**.

The logic is by entering *cheap* as a negative keyword (trigger), you are telling Google:

If they enter the word cheap, *they are NOT my customer, they are NOT going to convert, do NOT show my ad to them, I will NOT pay for that click!*

Here's a screenshot showing where to add Negative Keywords:

SEARCH KEYWORDS	NEGATIVE KEYWORDS	SEARCH TERMS ▾	
+			
☐ **Negative keyword** ↑			Added to
☐ cheap			Cat Emporium - Search Network
☐ cheap			Cat Emporium - Search Network › Cat Boarding

To add a negative keyword, just click on the blue plus sign, and type it in.

Where to Add Negative Keywords

Negative keywords can be added at two levels, so to speak:

- **Campaign Level** – if added here, then any Ad Group that "lives" in the Campaign is affected. Using our *cheap* example, then if someone entered the word *cheap* into Google as in *cheap cat boarding* or *cheap cat hotels*, then that would block the display of our ad for any of the dependent ad groups that live in the Cat Boarding San Francisco Campaign (i.e., the Ad Groups *Cat Boarding, Cat Hotels,* and *Cat Kennels*).
- **Ad Group Level** – if added here, then this impacts ONLY the Ad Group itself. So, if I add the negative keyword *cheap* to the Ad Group *cat boarding*, then if

someone enters *cheap cat boarding*, Google will NOT run our ad, but if they enter *cheap cat hotels*, then that Ad Group is not affected, and the ad will run.

Think of negative keywords as *stop words*. If the word is entered, then Google will NOT run your ad even if other words match.

Be sure on your Keyword Worksheet to identify any and all stop words that are 100% "not your customers." A detailed *negative keyword list* can save you a LOT of money in AdWords spend! You can read the AdWords help article on negative keywords at **http://jmlinks.com/25d**.

The Shared Library

If a keyword is always negative, across all your campaigns, I recommend drilling into the *shared library* (available by clicking first on the wrench at the top right and then clicking to "Negative Keyword Lists"). Here's a screenshot of where to find the *Shared Library > Negative keyword lists*:

I generally create a keyword list called "Universal Negatives" which contains the negative keywords I am absolutely, positively, 100% sure that if the user enters, I do NOT want my ad to be shown. Here's a screenshot:

When you click in, you simply add negative keywords using the same system of

"*cheap cat insurance*" = phrase match

cheap cat insurance = broad match

[cheap cat insurance] = exact match

I wouldn't worry about "+" signs here. In fact, because Google's incentive is to run your ads, I generally just enter the words with no quotes, no plus signs, and no brackets. So for instance, just enter:

cheap

free

Once you build out a universal negative keyword list, you want to add it to individual campaigns. To do this, here are the steps:

1. Click Campaigns on the left menu (to show all your Campaigns)
2. Select the Campaign to which you want to apply your "Universal Negatives" keyword list to.
3. Click Keywords on the left menu.
4. Click Negative Keywords on the top menu
5. Click the white plus sign in the blue circle.
6. Select "Use negative keyword list" and select your "Universal Negatives" list.
7. Click the blue SAVE on the bottom.

The easiest way to do this is to apply your "Universal Negative" list to each and every Campaign one by one. You can also select Campaigns and then apply the list to all of them at once; it isn't easy, as Google's made a convoluted mess of it in the New Interface. To learn how to do it, see the help file at **http://jmlinks.com/39s**. Once you've linked a Campaign to a negative keyword list, however, all you have to do is update the list, and it automatically updates every Campaign that is connected to it.

If, however, there are words that are negative only with respect to one Campaign or one Ad Group, then you can add them at that level by clicking on the Keywords tab at either the Campaign or Ad Group level. Here's a screenshot keywords at the Ad Group level, clearly showing how keywords can be added via a keyword list, or at the Ad Group or Campaign level:

NEGATIVE KEYWORDS

	Negative keyword ↑	Added to	Level
☐	free	Test - Cat Boarding › Cat Boarding	Ad group
☐	cheap	Test - Cat Boarding › Cat Boarding	Ad group
☐	cheap	Test - Cat Boarding	Campaign
☐	Felines	Test - Cat Boarding	Campaign
☐	feral	Test - Cat Boarding	Campaign
☐	free	Test - Cat Boarding	Campaign
☐	iguana	Test - Cat Boarding	Campaign
☐	Universal Negatives List	Test - Cat Boarding	Campaign

Now that you have your Campaigns and Ad Groups set up, plus you've added relevant keywords using plus signs, quote marks, and/or brackets as well as negative keywords at the Campaign, Ad Group, or Shared Library level, you're ready to write some ads. Ads "live" at the Ad Group level, and so by having tightly focused Ad Groups, we can now match *highly focused ads* to *highly focused Ad Groups* and *highly focused keywords* and *highly focused landing pages*.

The Purpose of an Ad

What's the purpose of an ad? If you answer, "to get clicks," well, you work for Google, or you haven't been paying attention. If you answer "to get clicks that lead to conversions," you're on the right track, and if you answer that the purpose of an ad is to:

Attract clicks from **relevant customers** that end in conversions and also to **repel** clicks from **non-customers**.

You get a gold star. We want to attract our customers and repel non-customers, sometimes derisively referred to as "tire kickers" on the old car lots.

INCLUDE KEYWORDS IN YOUR AD TEXT FOR BEST RESULTS

Let's investigate best practices for writing strong ad copy on AdWords. First, remember that AdWords Quality Score rewards a tight match between keywords and ads, so a major first principle is to:

include your **core keyword phrase** in your ad, preferably your ad headline.

You want to make it clear to the searcher that you have *exactly* what they want. Ads on AdWords in the new extended format include the following:

Headline 1 – 30 characters

Headline 2 – 30 characters

Description – 80 characters

Path ("Display URL") – 15 characters each

Second, in addition to including your target keyword in your ad headline, you want to have some **pizzazz** in your ad copy to "get the click," plus indicate how your product or service is unique and different. So for *cat boarding* in San Francisco, you might write an ad that looks like this:

Here's a screenshot of how you enter the ad into Google:

Final URL ↗

https://www.jasonmcdonald.org/ ⑦

Headline 1

Cat Boarding Experts. No Dogs. ⑦

30 / 30

Headline 2

San Francisco's #1 Cat Hotel. ⑦

29 / 30

jasonmcdonald.org / Cat-Boarding / San-Francisco

12 / 15   13 / 15

Description

Love your kitty? We do too. Experience the best cat boarding ⑦
in the City of SF.

79 / 80

Saving sends this new ad for review and removes your old ad.
Learn more

CANCEL   SAVE NEW AD

AdWords gives you a preview on the right of what your ad will look like on both mobile and desktop. Here's a screenshot of the mobile preview:

Note that you can put whatever you want in the Display URL field, and it's a best practice to include your keyword there as well. Hence, I wrote *Cat-Boarding/San-Francisco*. And note that this URL does *not* have actually to exist on your website; that's handled by the invisible "Final URL."

Here's an actual ad for *Cat Boarding in San Francisco*:

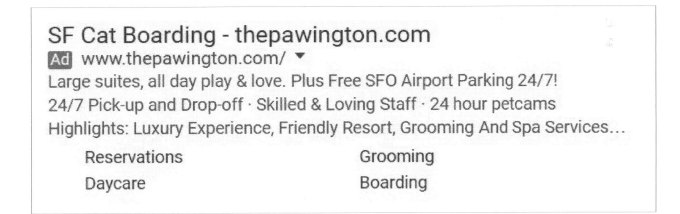

The first principle is to regurgitate the keyword phrase into the ad itself, preferably the headline as this ad does. The second is to have some pizzazz as in "Skilled and loving staff" and "24-hour petcams." Related to all this is to attract customers (preferably rich ones) with words like "Large suites" and "luxury experience" and implicitly repel certain types of undesirables (a.k.a., poor people) who can't afford a luxury experience. You can see how this Pawington ad is a true work of art: attracting the right kind of customers, repelling the others, and clearly stating its unique selling proposition. *Ah, AdWords poetry in action.*

Note as well that it's not shy. It's a bit brash, and it toots its own horn. If you don't toot your own horn, my High School English teacher once told me, no one will. So write your AdWords ads that you're #1, the best, on top, top-rated, luxury experience – whatever sells you as THE best match for what they are searching for (within reason).

Returning to The Pawington's ad, my main critique would be to use the Display URL to highlight cat boarding as in *pawington.com/cat-boarding/sf*. Google rewards ads that follow these principles with a better Quality Score, and the humans will more likely click on your ads if everything in them conveys that you have exactly what they're looking for; keywords and superlatives work together on this.

And, should you think I am against poor people, here's an ad for "hotels near me:"

Cheap Hotels Near Me - 60% Off Last Minute Hotels - hotwire.com
[Ad] www.hotwire.com/Hotels ▼
Travel Like A Baller, Don't Pay Like One. Never Pay Full Price On **Hotels** Again.
Chicago Hotels - from $54.00 - 3+ Star Hotels · More ▼

Book A Hot Rate® Hotel	Try Our Hot Rate® Flights
Bundle Up & Save More	Car Rentals From $8.99

This ad is thus attracting cheap or poor people, or what my Dad would call "frugal," and repelling people who want a top of the line experience. There's no wrong or right here – you're just aiming to attract your customers and repel spurious clicks.

For your **TODO**, do some relevant searches for your keywords and browse the ads that pop up. Do they attract? Do they repel? Do they inspire you to click? Do they clearly convey the business value proposition? Imitation is the highest form of flattery – just remember it's not only about *getting the click*, but it's also about *not getting the (wrong) click*, too. Read them out loud to your boss, your team, your sales staff, potential customers, or if all else fails, your Mom or Dad. Which ads spur you to click? Why?

This, in combination with tight Ad Groups focused on tight keywords, is the key to success on AdWords ad copywriting.

To sum up, the best ad copy:

1. Contains the target **keyword** in it, preferably in the headline.
2. Has some **pizzazz** explaining your brand and your unique selling proposition (USP)
3. **Attracts** your target customer yet **repels** non-customers.

All within the very tight character limits of Google AdWords. Good luck! (I know; It's like your worst High School English Poetry writing assignment has come true. But as you get into AdWords, you'll start to see that good ads are like Haiku's.) In fact, PPCHero had a contest for AdWords Haiku's, and here is the winner and a few runners-up:

New client, new goals

An empty canvas to fill

Words and ads, not paint

Click through rates are high

And conversion rates are low

Oh, CPA woes!

Fitting your message

Into just three lines. Is that

An ad or haiku?

Source: **http://jmlinks.com/39w**.

Quality Score: Don't Trust Google

Remember that Google gets paid *by the click* while you make money *by the conversion*. Google will want you to write ads that say things like *free cat boarding*, or *one night free* or something like that to encourage more clicks. In fact, if you watch Google videos or talk to Google AdWords technical support they will nearly ALWAYS tell you to write your ads in such a way as to maximize clicks.

> **VIDEO.** Watch a video from Google on how to write effective ads on AdWords at **http://jmlinks.com/26x**.

Good advice from Google on how to write ads? Yes, definitely, with the caveat that you want to make sure you've identified *negative keywords*, and thought about ways to *repel* non-customers. Don't believe everything you read or hear about ad copy, as many people think good ads get clicks when that's only half the story.

Attract & Repel: Striking a Balance

While it is true that higher click thru rates will generate a higher Quality Score, you have to strike a balance between ads that *get a lot of clicks* and ads that *generate a lot of conversions*.

STRIKE A BALANCE BETWEEN ADS THAT GET CLICKS AND ADS THAT GET CONVERSIONS

I tend to emphasize ads that focus on conversions, and not clicks. And I tend to use very focused *Ad Groups > Ads > Keywords* as "riches are in the niches" to improve my Quality Score. That's my style. I want every ad to match the search query tightly, so I'd write individual ads for:

Cat boarding

Luxury cat boarding

cat hotel

etc.

The tighter the match among Keyword > Ad Copy > Landing page, the better you will do.

You'll need to find your own style and workflow. Just be aware, however, that Google wants you to write ads that "get clicks," and I want you to write ads that "get conversions." So you will be penalized a bit by Google on Quality Score by using this strategy.

Quality Score

Once your Ad Groups are up and running, Google will give you some feedback on your Quality Score. Just drill into *Campaign > Ad Group > Keywords*. Next, hover your mouse over the dialogue box under Status, where is usually says *Eligible*. Here's a screenshot:

You can also enable the Quality Score column by clicking on *Columns (the three BAR icon) > Modify Columns > Attributes > Quality Score.* Here's a screenshot:

A quality score of 5 or higher is very good, and remember in some cases you may choose to accept a low-quality score for a high-value keyword for which you have written a powerful attract / repeal ad.

VIDEO. Watch an official video from Google on Quality Score in AdWords at **http://jmlinks.com/26u**.

Note: you sometimes may get a notification that your ad is / is not running for this keyword. We will discuss this in a few moments. Also, when your Ad Groups / Keywords are new, there may not be enough data to get a Quality Score reading.

Ambiguous Yet Important Keywords

Some keywords are unambiguous, and definitely your customer, as for example, *cat boarding*. Others are ambiguous – they contain both your customers and your non-customers. An example would be *pet boarding*. Some of those folks are *cat people*, some are *dog people*, and some are *exotic bird people*, but you only want the cat people.

What do you do?

You can either choose NOT to run on *pet boarding* entirely and run only on *cat boarding*. This makes sense if you have a very tight budget, or you want to be very conservative in terms of your AdWords strategy. (This is one of the most important reasons to have highly organized Campaigns and Ad Groups, so you can turn "on" and "off" keyword groups, leaving "on" your highest performing keywords at all times and turning "on" or "off" your lower performing keywords depending on your budget and other factors like seasonality).

But if you want to be more aggressive, you would want to run our ads on *pet boarding*, too. But we want to repel *dog people* and attract *cat people*. We can't use a negative keyword strategy as there is NOT a negative keyword; it's just *pet boarding*.

So what do we do? We write attract / repel ad copy that both includes the target keyword of *pet boarding* but clearly is all about *cats*:

New text ad

Final URL

https://www.jasonmcdonald.org/

Headline 1

Cat Boarding Hotel. No Dogs.

28 / 30

Headline 2

SF's #1 Pet Boarding for Cats.

30 / 30

Display path

jasonmcdonald.org / Cat-Boarding   / San-Francisco

12 / 15   13 / 15

Description

Love your kitty? We do too. Experience the best cat boarding in the City of SF.

79 / 80

Which shows on Google as:

Mobile

Cat Boarding Hotel. No Dogs. - SF's #1 Pet Boarding for Cats.

Ad jasonmcdonald.org/Cat-Boarding/San-Francisco

Love your kitty? We do too. Experience the best cat boarding in the City of SF.

The idea (and hope) being that dog people will be repelled by the phrase *No Dogs*, and NOT click on the ad. Now, relative to ads that say *pet boarding* and don't use repel, or establishments that board both cats and dogs, our ad will get fewer clicks and have a lower Quality Score, compelling us to bid somewhat higher. But what's the point in getting a click from a dog person, anyway, when he'll never convert because as soon as he lands on our website, he'll learn that we do NOT board dogs?

Attract /repel, in summary, is an important strategy to writing ads, especially when you confront **ambiguous keywords** that cannot be dealt with using negative keywords. I recommend you ignore the hit to your Quality Score and pay closer to attention to whether your ads are actually running, getting clicks, and getting conversions.

≫ USE AD EXTENSIONS

In addition to the headline, description, and path, ads on Google can also have "extensions." I recommend you populate them accordingly. I especially like the "Call extension" because if someone just calls right off the ad, you do not pay for that click! Ad extensions can be viewed or added by clicking into an Ad Group and then clicking Ads and extensions on blue on the left. Next, click Extensions in the middle tab. Here's a screenshot:

When you click on that, you should see a running list of all the ad extensions that are enabled for that Ad Group. It's a little confusing because when you click on the pencil to edit one extension, Google reminds you that by editing it, you will be editing it on all other Ad Groups or Campaigns that share this extension. (Extensions can function at the Account, Campaign, and/or Ad Group level).

To add a new Ad Extension, just click the white plus sign in the blue circle, and you'll get to choose what type to add:

ADS	EXTENSIONS

✕

+ Sitelink extension

+ Callout extension

+ Structured snippet extension

+ Call extension

+ Message extension

+ Location extension

+ Affiliate location extension

+ Price extension

+ App extension

+ Review extension

+ Promotion extension

We'll overview what each means in a moment, but for now, just click on Sitelink Extension, which is the most common type. You can select which level – Account, Campaign, or Ad Group to add the extension to. Here's a screenshot:

Next, create your Sitelink extension (or other extension) by filling out the required field. Here's a screenshot:

Add sitelink extension

Add to

Account ▾

Extension

◉ Create new   ○ Use existing

Sitelink text

                                                    0 / 25

Description line 1 (optional)

                                                    0 / 35

Description line 2 (optional)

                                                    0 / 35

Final URL   ⊘

⌄ Sitelink URL options

⌄ Advanced options

Just to be clear, remember that Ad Extensions do not always show, but if you do some highly competitive searches like *auto insurance* or *car insurance*, you can usually see them in action. Here's a sample ad for hair transplant that has extensions:

$6/Graft ARTAS Hair Transplant - Special Valid This Month Only
[Ad] www.precisionmdca.com/Hair-Transplant ▾ (916) 340-8914
No Scarring & Natural Results. Free Consultation. Call Now to Claim This Rate!
New ARTAS Hair Transplant · Doctor Owned & Operated · State-of-the-art Lasers
Services: Acne Scar Removal, Botox, Juvederm, Hair Transplants, Liposuction, Brazilian Butt Lift, Tattoo...
Meet Dr. Khattab · Why Precision MD?

The ad extensions are things like the phone number *(916) 340-8914,* the non-clickable text underneath the ad such as *State-of-the-art Lasers,* and the sitelinks (clickable) extensions such as *Meet Dr. Khattab.*

Available extensions are:

Sitelinks – these are blue-highlighted bits of text that can appear below an ad, and link to specific subsections of your website such as "contact us" or "cat grooming," etc.

Callouts – these are non-clickable text elements that can appear below an ad, usually meant to "call out" something special such as "Valentine's Day Specials" or "ask about our kitty services".

Structured Snippets – you select a predefined header like "Product" or "Service category" and then add callouts to specific subsections of your website.

Call extensions – these allow your phone number to appear in ads.

Message extensions – these appear on mobile phone ads, and allow customers to text message you directly from the ad.

Location – this extension type allows users to see your store's physical address.

Affiliate location – similar to the above.

Price extensions – allow users to browse products and prices in an ad, and then click directly to them on your website.

App extensions – allow you to link from your ad to your mobile app for download and installation.

Reviews – this extension type allows you to pull reviews from third party websites and thereby enable review stars on your ads.

Promotion extension – this extension allows you to enter a "sale" or "promotion" such as a $ off an item.

To read the official Google help file on ad extensions, visit **http://jmlinks.com/23q**.

Here's another screenshot of an ad with clickable sitelink extensions:

So *Get a Quote* and *BIG Savings* go to unique URLs on Geico.com, plus they have their 888 number in the ad, too. And here's a screenshot of an ad with a location extension and stars (coming from their Google reviews):

Notice how DeVry has added their phone number of 855-604-8442 as a call extension, and how the location extension shows their address.

And here's a screenshot with a review extension, again getting the advertiser those nifty, eye-catching stars:

Warehouse Industrial Fans - In Stock. Ships Today - uline.com
Ad www.uline.com/Warehouse-**Fans** ▾
4.6 ★★★★★ rating for uline.com
ULINE - Over 31,000 Items in Stock. Huge Catalog! Same Day Shipping.
Fast Delivery · 11 Locations · 31,000+ Products
Ratings: Shipping 9.5/10 - Quality 8.5/10 - Website 8.5/10 - Selection 8.5/10 - Add-on services 8/10

Floor Fans   Pedestal Fans
Wall Mount Fans   Drum Fans

Notice how this ad has a display URL that contains a keyword (*Warehouse Fans*), as well as call out extensions and structured snippet extensions.

Automated Extensions

Finally, Google has rolled out a new type of extension called *Automated Extensions* which are, automatically, generated by Google. You can read about them at **http://jmlinks.com/39t**. You can opt out of Automated Extensions by clicking into the Automated Extensions tab, and then the three dots at the right, then Advanced Options. You then have to go through each type and opt out. Here's a screenshot:

How would you like automated extensions to work in your account?

○ Use all automated extensions that typically boost ads' performance ⑦
Best option for most advertisers

◉ Turn off specific automated extensions
Not recommended because it could negatively affect your ads' performance

Currently off for this account:

Dynamic sitelinks ✕

Turn off automated extension

Select which extension to turn off
Choose an extension type ▼

TURN OFF

DONE   CANCEL

Check your Automated Extensions periodically and see if you think they are working for you. Because Google provides so little data on what they look like and what's happening with them, **I recommend you turn them off**. The most common types are:

Dynamic sitelinks

Structured snippets

In summary, I do recommend that you set up relevant ad extensions to your ads, but have an attract / repel frame of mind. You might not want to emphasize a *free consult* if *free consult* is likely to attract poor people or those who are not likely to convert! You might not want an ad extension that emphasizes your *cat grooming* services if those services are likely to generate clicks but are not strong revenue-generators for your company. And generally I don't trust Google's Artificial Intelligence enough to write my own extensions, so I disable the Automated Extensions feature.

» Follow C/E/A on Landing Pages

What happens after the click? Well, they "land" on your website. There are some best practices when it comes to landing pages for AdWords, starting with a tight match between the keyword query and the landing page.

Accordingly,

keyword group = Ad Group on AdWords = specific landing page

So, we'd have:

cat boarding = Ad Group on cat boarding = specific landing page on cat boarding

vs.

cat grooming = Ad Group on cat grooming = specific landing page on cat grooming

vs.

pet boarding = Ad Group on pet boarding = specific landing page on pet boarding

Note how we aren't lazy, and we don't let reality confuse us! We have a tight match between keywords and landing pages.

Don't Make Customers (or Google) Think!

We have a page specific to **cat boarding** even though, technically speaking, we could send the *cat boarding* people to our *pet boarding* page or our home page since "in reality" that's the same thing. But we don't want to "make our customers think" – we want the *cat boarding* people to see immediately that we board cats, and the *pet boarding* people to see, first, yes we board pets, and secondly, we focus on cats. We also want the reward to our Quality Score by having a tight focus <u>at the keyword level</u> between the keyword query and the landing page. Don't make Google think, either!

It's not generally a good idea to send everyone to your homepage, and certainly not a good idea to make users hunt for information. They'll click, and bounce, rather than click, and convert. In fact, Google strongly emphasizes that one element of Quality Score is a keyword-matching landing page.

Generally speaking, therefore, your **TODO** is to map out your Keywords to your Ad Groups and your Ad Groups to your landing pages and build a one-to-one correlation between *Core Keywords* to *Ad Groups* to *landing pages*.

C/E/A Methodology for Landing Pages

In terms of landing page design, you want to use the C/E/A methodology, which stands for Confirm / Engage / Act. Basically, if the search query is *cat boarding*, then when the user lands on your landing page in the top left corner, she should see an image of a happy cat being boarded, and the phrase she just entered ("cat boarding). That's your "**C**" for Confirmation Zone.

Next, moving from left to right, top to bottom, she should read some content that explains why your establishment is the best place to board a cat in San Francisco. Awards, user reviews, statistics, etc., are great here. This is your "**E**" for "Engagement" zone.

Finally, to the right, but above the fold, the desired action should be apparent. This is your "**A**" for Action zone. A common action is "free consult" or "request a quote" or something like that. Note that in contrast to writing the ad, here you want to convert EVERYONE who lands on your website into an email inquiry (or e-Commerce transaction), as you have already paid for the click, so you want to grab each and every lead.

Attract / repel refers ONLY to ad copy, not to the landing page experience.

Here's a screenshot with the three zones for C/confirm, E/ngage, and A/ct outlined on the landing page for ZOHO for the search query *CRM Software* into Google:

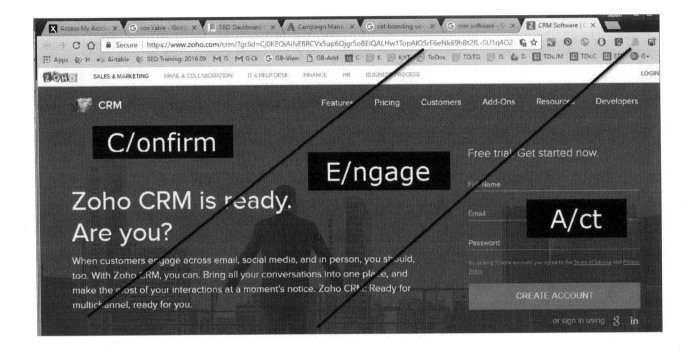

And here's the Geico landing page for the search query, *motorcycle insurance*, again with the C/, E/, and A/ zones clearly marked for you.

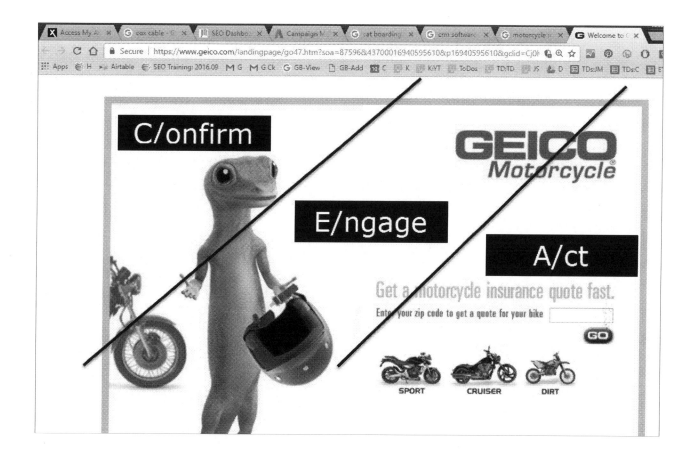

Your **TODOS** here are to a) do relevant search queries in your industry and evaluate competitor landing pages using this C/E/A methodology, and b) look at your own landing pages with an eye to C/E/A.

1. Does the **top left** corner **confirm** that the customer who just clicked from Google has landed on a relevant website that offers what he wants?
2. Does the **middle engage** the customer by explaining the offer and validating that you are a company that can be trusted?
3. Does the **right** have a defined **action** such as request a free consultation, download a software demo, or buy something on an e-Commerce site?

And, is all the human-critical information "above the fold?" Don't make them think. Don't make them hunt. Don't make them nervous. Confirm you have what they want, you're a fantastic choice, and make it easy for them to see the next step.

As for allowing navigation to your homepage, and other web pages, some people advocate "locking in" the customer and others say you should at least allow navigation to the home page. My advice is to allow navigation to your home page, and website. Many customers will want to "check you out" and will want to browse your site, even if they land on a clear landing page.

Thus, while I recommend using the C/E/A methodology for your AdWords landing pages, I realize that many customers will nonetheless browse your website. We can use Google Analytics to track user behavior and view the conversion rates of any customers who come from AdWords. (Note: others will advocate that your landing page "lock in" customers, preventing them from scrolling anywhere other than either forward to your action or backward to Google. That's not my style, but it's a respectable position in AdWords strategy).

The bottom line is that each landing page, and your website as a whole, should clearly

- **CONFIRM** that users have landed on a website the offers what they just searched for
- **ENGAGE** them with information, facts, reviews, and other trust indicators that validate your company, products, and services as trustworthy and high quality, and
- have an **ACTION** such as an e-Commerce purchase or free consult / free download that makes the next step easy to see and find.

» SET YOUR BIDS

Advertisers pay by click on AdWords. In AdWords, you set your bid strategy at the Campaign Level. Click on your *Campaign* and then the *Settings* tab on the left. Find Bidding in the center of the screen and click the down chevron to view it.

Here's a screenshot:

Bidding	Manual CPC
	☐ Enable Enhanced CPC ⑦
	AdWords automatically adjusts your manual bids to try to maximize conversions
	Change bid strategy ⑦

Click on Change bid strategy, and AdWords will show you your options:

Manual CPC

Change bid strategy ⑦

Automated bid strategies

Target CPA

Target ROAS

Maximize clicks

Maximize conversions

Target search page location

Target outranking share

Enhanced CPC

Manual bid strategies

Manual CPC

Below, I explain what each means, and indicate in italics my opinion of each option:

Target CPA. Use this if you have an e-Commerce site and have enabled conversion tracking. This allows you to set a target Cost Per Acquisition. If for example, you know that you make $1.00 per widget, you can set a target CPA of $1.00 and AdWords will do the calculations for you of how many clicks vs. how many bounces and what your best CPC is (which will be lower than $1.00 because not everyone converts). *Recommended for e-Commerce websites that have a sufficient spend and have sufficient sales per click.*

Target ROAS. This is similar to CPA but works across an entire account to attempt to maximize your ROAS (Return on Ad Spend). *Not recommended for small advertisers, and works only if you have conversion tracking running well.*

Maximize clicks. Here you provide Google your budget, and Google attempts to maximize your bids within that budget. You can also set a "bid max" to set a maximum CPC you are willing to run. *Not recommended, as I find better results with Manual CPC, but OK if you set a "bid max."*

Target outranking share. This bidding strategy pits you against a competitor and attempts to outrank their ad. *Not recommended, as essentially you are paying for a "bidding war" within AdWords!*

Target search page location. Use this if you want to always show near the top of a page, but aren't very concerned about the cost per click you'll pay. *Not recommended, as you are usually overcharged.*

Enhanced CPC. Here, you have enabled conversion tracking, but you bid by click, allowing AdWords to boost your bids up on clicks it thinks are likely to lead to a conversion. *Recommended strategy if you have conversion tracking enabled.*

Manual CPC. Here, you manually set your bids as the maximum you are willing to pay for a click. *Recommended strategy.*

You can read the official Google help file at **http://jmlinks.com/23x**, but it's not very clear and mixes bidding on the Search Network with bidding on the Display Network.

VIDEO. Watch a video from Google on bid strategies in AdWords at **http://jmlinks.com/26y**.

For most advertisers, the enhanced CPC or manual CPC will yield the best return on investment, especially if you monitor your bids and conversions on a weekly basis. Simply select the appropriate bid strategy at the Campaign Level, and you're all set to go to the next level, Ad Groups, where bidding actually occurs. I recommend you start with Manual CPC.

Bidding at the Ad Group Level

While the bid *strategy* is set at the Campaign level, the actual *bid per click* is set at the Ad Group level or at the Keyword level. We'll assume you've built out your Campaign and have at least one Group in it, and have written ads in that group. AdWords will have forced you to enter a bid at the beginning, but now go back and edit this bid.

The easiest way to set your bids is to click into the bid on the Default Max CPC column at the Group level. Here's a screenshot:

		Ad group	Status	Default max. CPC
		Plumber	Eligible	$10.01 (enhanced)
		Plumbing	Eligible	$9.01 (enhanced)
		Emergency	Eligible	$12.01 (enhanced)

AD GROUPS   AUCTION INSIGHTS

Whatever you set as the maximum CPC bid here controls the dependent bid at the keyword level. So all keywords in the "Plumber" Ad Group will be set at $10.01 CPC maximum bid.

What to Bid at First?

When starting a new *Campaign > Ad Group*, I recommend you bid on the high side, higher than you'd expect or be willing to pay in the long run. To estimate a good starting bid, go to the **Keyword Planner** under the **Tools** menu in AdWords, enter your keyword, and bid at least as high as the suggested bid. Here's a screenshot

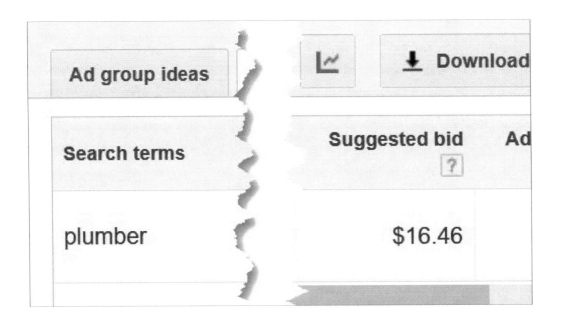

So I'd bid at least $16.46 per click to get started with *plumber*. However, as you can see from the previous screenshot, I have reduced my bid over time to $12.01. This is because the Campaigns and Ad Groups are now highly optimized and running well, so – over time – I have been able to reduce the bids and still get good performance. (More on this later).

But when you're starting a brand new Ad Group, **bid high** as you must get the ads actually to run. Then **monitor closely** and notch down your bids slowly until you get the ads to show at least 85% of the time (as expressed by the Search Impression Share) and you have a position of < 4 on the page. (More on this later).

You can also use the SERPS.com keyword research tool at **http://jmlinks.com/23y** to get CPC / bid estimates.

Set Bids at the Keyword Level

You can also set your bids at the keyword level if there are certain phrases that you want to bid higher than for the Ad Group as a whole. To do this, click on the keywords tab, scroll down to a keyword, and then enter a bid.

Here's a screenshot, showing how I have bid up my bid on "best plumber" at $12.01:

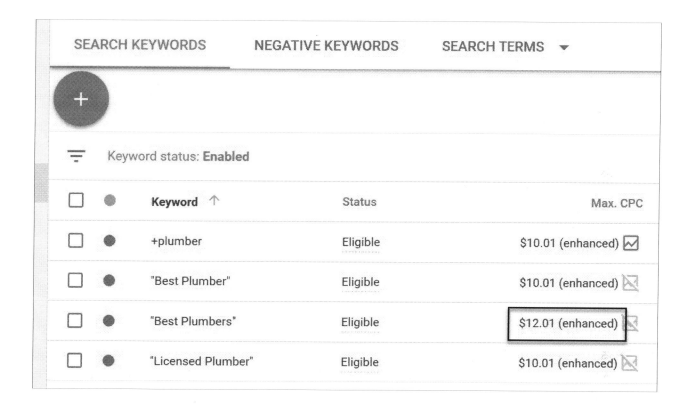

If you set a bid at the keyword level, remember that this overrides the Ad Group level. So if you increase your Ad Group bid, then the bid at the keyword group stays in charge, even it's a lower amount.

Here's a tip to track who set which bids. If you're working as a team, or with a client, have one person bid as a .01, another as a .02, and a third as a .03, or even / odd. This way, you can see who bid what. So, I always bid .01, so I can tell that the bid of $5.01 was set by me, vs. the client bid which might be $5.00 and a bid by Gloria, who works for me, that would be $5.02. These pennies don't do anything to the bids in any serious sense; they just tell us who set the bids on a team project.

We'll return to bids after we jump over to Campaigns, as after a few days or a week, you want to go back and monitor your bids, bidding them up or reducing them down until you find the best bid per click for return on investment.

» SET LOGICAL CAMPAIGN SETTINGS

Because AdWords is an interrelated "whole" and yet composed of hierarchical "parts," it's useful to zig and zag between the parts. So, return to your Campaign Settings, and review them by clicking on the *Settings* tab, with an eye to whether your Campaign settings reflect aspects of the real world such as geotargets, budget, etc.

Click on the Here are the basic settings for each Campaign in your AdWords account that are relevant on the Search Network:

- **Goal**. If you select a Goal, AdWords will give you suggestions based on the Goal as you work through the process. I never enable this, as I find the suggestions useless, misleading, or just annoying, but it doesn't hurt to enable a goal.
- **Networks**. Here you select Search Network (pre-selected by the above choice). If you want to run on sites like Yelp, Xfinity, Earthlink, etc., then choose Google search partners. If you want to run only on Google, then uncheck the Search Partners box. Again, never mix a Display Network and a Search Network campaign!
- **Locations**. Here is where you set the geotarget or location target for your Campaign. We'll discuss this in a moment; but just realize that you can Geotarget everyone who lives, for example, within a 10-mile radius of Tulsa, Oklahoma, or in Zipcode 94111.
- **Languages**. You can select the desired language (e.g., English).
- **Bidding**. As explained above, you can set a bid strategy ranging from a fully automated strategy to manual CPC. For most advertisers, I recommend *Manual CPC, Manual CPC + Enhanced CPC,* or *Enhanced CPC* as the best bid strategies.
- **Budget**. Set your daily maximum budget here. Again, this is controlled at the Campaign level and controls the budget for all dependent Ad Groups.
- **Dynamic Search Ads**. Use this feature if you want Google to spider your website and automatically create ads for you. Are you CRAZY? Never enable this feature unless you just want to shovel money from you to Google. It's terrible.
- **Additional Settings**
  - **Location Options.** Generally, the default is fine. I'll explain in a moment what these mean in special circumstances.

- Campaign URL options. Use this if you have special parameters in your URLs (as may occur in e-Commerce).
- IP Exclusions. Use this if you know certain IP's are bad (e.g., those of competitors). Rarely used as it is too difficult to maintain manually.

⏩ CHOOSE YOUR GEOTARGET SETTINGS WISELY

You can show your ads only to people searching in or about a specific location (e.g., San Francisco). This is called *location targeting* or *geotargeting*. It's one of the most powerful advantages of AdWords over SEO (Search Engine Optimization).

To set up or adjust your location targeting, go to *Campaigns* and click on *Settings* and then open up the *Locations* tab in the center. (It's confusing. Do not click on Locations on the left menu as that is only a report as to where your clicks are coming from. Be sure to select the Locations tab in the Center.). Here's a screenshot:

Campaign name	Cat Emporium - Search Network	⌄
Campaign status	● Enabled	⌄
Goal	No goal selected	⌄
Networks	Google Search Network, Search partners	⌄

Locations — Select locations to target ⑦
- ○ All countries and territories
- ○ United States and Canada
- ○ United States
- ◉ Enter another location

Targeted locations (1)   Reach ⑦ ✖
San Francisco, California, United States city   10,200,000 ✖

🔍 Enter a location to target or exclude   Advanced search

CANCEL   SAVE

This means that the Campaign "Cat Emporium – Search Network" will show ads only to people physically in San Francisco or who append the phrase "San Francisco" to their search.

Let's review geotargeting in detail.

The best way to set or revisit your geotargeting settings is to click on **Advanced Search** as indicated in blue above. This pops up a map. Next, you have two ways to go about setting location targeting. If you select the circle "Location," then you can just enter states, cities, or even zip codes to target. Here's a screenshot showing zip code 74135:

If you select TARGET that means show your ad to people in that zip code. If you select EXCLUDE, that means do not show your ad to people in that zip code. In this method, you can manually enter cities, states, and zip codes to target or exclude for a given Campaign.

The second method is to select "Radius" in the circle. This is useful if you want to target people who are within, say, a 20-mile radius of San Francisco, California. Here's a screenshot:

And here's a screenshot of what the map looks like with a 10-mile radius around San Francisco:

You can see that we'd reach some people across the Bay in Oakland, and Alameda, as well as north into Marin County.

Excluding Geographic Areas like Cities, States, or ZIP Codes

Let's discuss *exclusions*. You can use the geotarget feature to include "in" cities, states, zip codes, etc., but you can also use them exclude "out" cities, states, ZIP codes, etc. These function like *negative keywords* and block your ads from showing at all.

Why might you do this? For example, consider a scenario where you are a Napa Valley, California, vineyard that sells wine over the Internet, across the entire United States. So you want to use AdWords to reach people searching for "buy wine online,' or "best cabernets from Napa Valley," etc. AdWords is a fantastic choice to reach these wine connoisseurs who want to buy California Napa Valley wines over the Internet. However, it is illegal to buy wine online in Utah, Oklahoma, Arkansas, Mississippi, Delaware, Rhode Island, and Alabama.

By using the geotarget / exclude feature, you can exclude showing ads to people in these states. Simply go to *Advanced Search >Search*, and enter the state names, then select *exclude*. Here's a screenshot, showing a search for Oklahoma. If you look closely, you'll see Alabama has been grayed out, as I already excluded it:

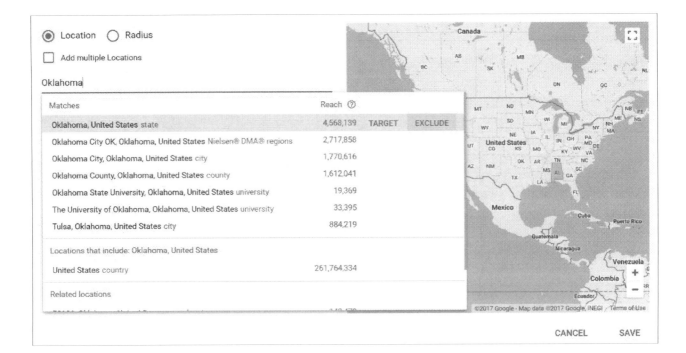

In this way, you'd set your Geotarget to United States, and then exclude states like Oklahoma and Alabama which do not allow wine shipments. There's no point in paying for someone in these states to click on your ad only to find out that they can't use your service.

Poor vs. Rich People by Geography

You can think "out of the box" when it comes to geotargeting. So, if for example, your target customers tend to live in one ZIP code, and your non-customers live in another, you can include "in" your target customers and exclude "out" your non-target customers. It may be politically incorrect to point this out but (unfortunately) in our great nation, it is often true that poor people tend to live in certain zip codes and rich people in others. By using geotargeting in AdWords, you can include "in" rich people and exclude "out" poor people based on geotargets.

GEOTARGET "IN" AND GEOTARGET "OUT"

Rich people tend to live in certain ZIP codes and poor people in others. (You can check USA incomes by zip codes out at **http://jmlinks.com/23z**). By using geotargeting, we could exclude the poor zip codes and target only people in rich zip codes. Other ways to use geotargeting can be including "in" people in a commute zone (e.g., from Oakland to San Francisco), and including "out" people outside of a commute zone (e.g., the more difficult commute from Marin County into San Francisco).

Your **TODO** here is to identify communities you want to geotarget "in" and any you want to geotarget "out," and then map those to your individual Campaigns.

Advanced Location Options

Finally, click back up to your Campaign settings, find Additional Settings, and just below that click on *Location options*. Here's a screenshot:

Here you will find the following cryptic language from Google:

> People in, who show interest in, your targeted locations (recommended)
>
> People in your targeted locations
>
> People searching for your targeted locations

The way to think about this is by asking where the person is who is your target. A person physically in San Francisco who types in "cat boarding" is definitely a target, but so is a person who works across the Bay in Oakland who types in "San Francisco cat boarding." That's why the default setting includes "interest in" your target location.

You'd only override these settings if, for some reason, you want to physically constrict it to people physically in the target but exclude those who include it by typing in the city name. A scenario might be a San Francisco bike rental company that only wants to target people who are truly in San Francisco and ready to bike vs. people in Milwaukee who might be planning a trip and are just looking around (but not yet physically in the City). So they would selection "People in your targeted location," and the ads would thus show if, and only if, the person is physically in the City of San Francisco. Get it?

For most of us, the default setting is fine, however. To be on the safe side, you could also enter the keyword *+cat +boarding +san +francisco* into AdWords to be sure to capture search queries that are clearly looking for cat boarding in the city of San Francisco.

VIDEO. Watch a video from Google on how to set location targeting in AdWords at **http://jmlinks.com/26k**.

►► MONITOR YOUR BIDS AND PERFORMANCE

Chapter 7 goes into more detail on how to monitor AdWords for return on investment, but for now, let's overview the basics of monitoring your performance. We'll leave aside *conversion tracking*, but if you can, you should connect Google Analytics to AdWords, and make sure that it is tracking conversions (e.g., purchases at an e-Commerce website, or completed website feedback forms) as soon as possible.

When you're just getting started, I'd recommend keeping a very close eye on AdWords, on at least a daily basis at first. Then, after a week or ten days of data, it's time to analyze your performance.

Account Level

Select the Campaigns Tab to compare Campaigns to each other. Note: essentially here you are at the Account "level," and looking "down" to your Campaigns. Here's a screenshot:

		Campaign ↑	Budget	Impr.	Interactions	Interaction rate	Avg. cost	Cost
☐	●	Books - Search Network	$100.01/day	121,172	6,446 clicks	5.32%	$2.13	$13,733.62
☐	●	Cat Emporium - Search Network	$1.01/day	619	7 clicks	1.13%	$3.95	$27.64
☐	●	Jason McDonald	$100.00/day	30,787	451 clicks	1.46%	$11.11	$5,008.99
☐	●	Stanford in CA	$50.01/day	1,042	81 clicks	7.77%	$5.78	$468.45
		Total: Filtered campaigns		153,620	6,985 clicks	4.55%	$2.75	$19,238.70
		Total: Account	$251.03/day	38,950,729	33,422 clicks, views	0.09%	$2.34	$78,203.50
		Total: Search		2,828,588	19,328 clicks	0.68%	$3.02	$58,395.53
		Total: Display		36,005,190	13,459 clicks, views	0.04%	$1.45	$19,555.05
		Total: Video		116,951	635 views	0.54%	$0.40	$252.92

On the top right, select the time period (e.g., last month, last week, etc.). AdWords will then give you an organized look at your Campaigns. You can select "All enabled

162 | P a g e

Campaigns" to see just the Campaigns that are running by clicking the filter icon on the right (it looks like an upside down triangle).

Here's what the **default** columns mean:

Campaign. This is the name of your campaign.

Budget. This is your budget maximum per day.

Impressions. These are the number of times your ads were shown.

Interactions. For most of us, this is just clicks.

Interaction Rate (Click thru rate). This is the number of clicks divided by the number of impressions expressed as a percentage. Generally speaking, anything 1% or higher is good.

Avg Cost. This is your average cost-per-click (CPC). Lower is better, of course.

Cost. This is your total cost spent during the time period.

Unfortunately, Google has goofed this all up in the New Interface, so I recommend you drill into columns and disable some of the goofy ones and enable ones that make more sense. Click on the columns icon on the middle right. It is three black bars, like this:

That then opens up a "Modify columns for campaigns" box. Open up each of these, and I recommend you enable the following columns:

Performance. Uncheck the defaults, and check *Impr.* (Impressions), *Clicks, Avg CPC, Cost, CTR,* and *Avg. Position.*

Conversions. If you have conversions enabled, select *Conversions,* and *Cost / conv*

Competitive Metrics. Enable *Search impr. share* (SIS).

On the far right, you can drag up or down each column and order them in any way you like. I usually think of it as a process from showing on Google to getting the conversion, so I order them:

Cost, Impr., Search impr. share, Avg. pos, Clicks, CTR, Avg CPC, Conversions, and Cost/conv.

Once you've checked all the ones you want, click "Save your column set," and give it a name such as My Columns. Hit SAVE & APPLY and Google will apply this column set. Note: you have to do this at both the Campaign and Ad Group level, but once you save a column set you can turn it on / off by clicking on the Column icon.

Bids and SIS Scores

Return to the Campaign Level, where you're looking down at your Ad Groups, by clicking on the top breadcrumb trail navigation. You want to get back "up" to the Campaign level, so you can see your multiple Ad Groups. Enable the same columns as indicated above, and save them as "My Columns." Here's a screenshot:

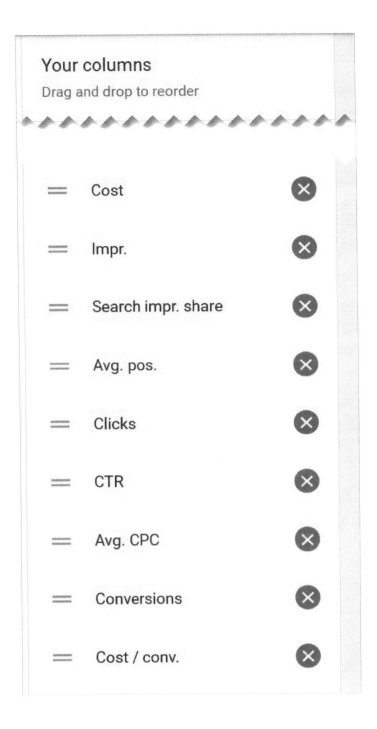

This then outputs from the Campaign level looking "down" at the Ad Groups inside the Campaign like:

Ad group	Cost	Impr.	Search impr. share	Avg. pos.	Clicks	CTR	Avg. CPC
Plumber	$1,390.25	8,128	69.33%	1.9	218	2.68%	$6.38
Plumbing	$515.94	2,152	83.87%	2.2	70	3.25%	$7.37
Emergency	$80.66	96	94.06%	1.8	7	7.29%	$11.52
Reviews	$21.27	86	96.63%	1.2	2	2.33%	$10.63
Commercial	$11.66	81	81.63%	1.7	1	1.23%	$11.66
Residential	$10.18	18	94.74%	1.7	1	5.56%	$10.18
Plumber Exact	$0.00	4	100.00%	1.3	0	0.00%	$0.00
Total: Ad groups	$2,029.96	10,565	72.38%	1.9	299	2.83%	$6.79
Total: Campaign	$2,029.96	10,565	72.38%	1.9	299	2.83%	$6.79

Let's go over what this all means. Again, remember, we are in a Campaign and looking "down" at the Ad Groups that "live" inside a Campaign. AdWords is a hierarchy.

Ad Group. This is the name you give to each Ad Group. I usually give it a name to reflect the core keyword such as *plumber*, or *emergency* for *emergency plumbing* in the above example.

Cost. This is the spend for the time period (usually one month, or month-to-date), whatever you select in the top right for time.

Impr. These are the impressions for the time period, i.e., how many times your ad was shown. 8,128 means that that Ad Group's ads were shown 8,128 times during the month.

Search impr. share (SIS). This is a very useful metric. This shows the percent time your ad was shown vs. the eligible impressions. So if it was 100%, your ad showed all the time; if it was 69%, it showed 69% of the time and was not showing 31% of the time. You want this to be > 85% to be running "full blast."

Avg. pos. This is your ad's position on the page, counting from the top. You want this to be < 5, meaning you ranked in the top three or four positions. You want this to be around three, though it's hard to hit. (*More on this in a moment*).

Clicks. These are the number of clicks your Ad Group's ads received during the time period.

CTR. This is your click thru rate, calculated by impressions/clicks. Higher is better, and you want this to be > 2% in general. Anything > 2% is good, >5% is very good. It speaks to how exciting and "on target" your ad headline and copy was vs. the search query.

Avg. CPC. This is the average price you paid per click. Lower is obviously better.

Conversions and Conversion Rate. If you have conversion tracking on, you can see the number of conversions and the conversion rate. This tells you that they not only clicked through but actually "converted," meaning they did what you identified as a goal such as an e-Commerce purchase or a registration or a sales lead.

Threading the Needle

AdWords is full of trade-offs. So, assuming you did a good job on identifying high value, transactional keywords and you matched those keywords to Ad Groups, let's discuss threading the needle. You want to maximize your return on ad investment by getting the most qualified clicks to your website to generate the most conversions at the lowest cost per conversion.

A perfect Ad Group would hit approximately:

An **SIS** or **Search Impression Share** of > 85%, meaning your ads were showing nearly all the time.

A **position** of < 5, meaning your ad showed in the top three or four positions, preferably three or four as you pay a premium to show at the very top.

A **CTR** of > 2%, meaning people liked your ads and clicked through on them.

A **good conversion rate** and **cost per conversion**. This varies greatly based on what you are selling, but you want not only clicks but ads that convert. You can't make a blanket statement as what percent is a good one, as a conversion rate for a cheap purse may be very different from an expensive purse and even more different from a cruise to Italy.

Adjusting if Your Ads Are Not Showing

What do you do if your ads aren't showing? For example, you have an SIS that's 25%, or a position that's 6? What are your mechanisms to improve things?

Focus. If you haven't tightly focused your Ad Groups to a specific core keyword, that will show up as poor performance. Tighten your focus.

Bids. You can bid up your bid per click until you get the SIS to be > 85%, as nothing works if your ads don't show.

Ad Copy. If your ads are not showing (i.e., they have a poor quality score), rewrite them to include the keywords in the ad headline and text. Give them some pizzazz, and promise something like a "free consult" or "free download." (This will improve the CTR and improve the ad being shown).

Geotarget. If you are running out of budget, it's better to narrow your geotarget and get the SIS > 85% than to spread yourself too thin and be SIS < 85%. Google penalizes ads that run haphazardly, so I always strive to get the SIS > 85% by tuning things up.

Poor Conversions. Here your problem isn't with Google, but rather with your landing page. You're getting clicks, but they're not converting. Assuming your keyword patterns are tight (i.e., transactional, relevant searches), then work on your landing page experience. What will get users to convert to your desired goal once they land on your website? What's fouling it up?

Bid Tweaking if Your Ads are Showing

If your ads are performing well, meaning your SIS is greater than 85%, your CTR is greater than 2%, and your ad position is less than 5, then I recommend lowering your bids every week until your SIS drops below 85% and your ad position deteriorates below the top four. Assuming you have chosen high-value, transactional keywords and your bid per click isn't terribly high, you want to run "full blast." Every time someone enters a relevant query into Google, you want your ad to show.

Now, here's the rub. The official propaganda from Google will tell you that no matter what you bid, you just pay .01 more than the person below you (with some wrinkles for relative Quality Score). So why not just set a high bid and let AdWords run on autopilot? Well, for one, if everyone did that, then there'd be a bidding war to the top, much to the benefit of Google.

Yet this is what the official propaganda implies. Just set a high bid, and you'll only pay .01 more than the advertiser below you.

> **VIDEO.** Watch a video from Google's Chief Economist, Hal Varian, on how bidding works in AdWords at **http://jmlinks.com/39u**.

With all due respect to Hal Varian, I would like to argue that this is just so much rubbish. This is not my experience with Google over many years and many different clients. You can't and shouldn't just leave AdWords on autopilot, trusting you'll only pay .01 more than the advertiser below you.

> *If you bid too high, Google just takes your extra money despite what you read in the official help files.*

In my experience, it seems that you can often get *more* clicks and certainly *more* clicks at *cheaper* cost by gradually reducing your bid, and keeping an eye on your SIS to be greater than 85% and your position to be less than five. It's sort of like throttling an airplane, as you're trying to reduce your bid to discover the "real" cost per click yet maintaining an 85% SIS and a < 5 position.

> **TODO.** Gradually reduce your bid per click, until you fall below an SIS > 85%, a position of about 3, and a decent click through rate. If you SIS goes below 85%, you're bidding too low, so raise your bid If your position goes to 1 or 2, you're probably bidding too high. So raise and lower your bid until you find the "sweet spot" where you run at the cheapest cost but show all the time.

It's hard to hit the perfect "sweet spot" here, but it's very important to realize that – despite what Google tells you – you want to bid *down* over time. You can't "trust Google" to get you the cheapest cost per click. In fact, I have had advertisers who get *more* clicks and a *higher* SIS by bidding *low* than by bidding *high* – despite what the official Google propaganda says about just paying .01 more than the advertiser below you in the auction.

Indeed, even if you are all by yourself on a keyword query, there seem to be **minimum bids** set in AdWords. If you bid too low, your ads do not appear. If you bid too high, Google seems to just take that extra bid money, despite what Hal Varian says in the official video. (You can read an official Google "explanation" of this at **http://jmlinks.com/39x**, which I just think is poppycock and propaganda).

> **Trust but verify**. Monitor and change your bids, paying attention to SIS, CTR, and Position (and conversions). Don't take what Google says, officially, as the Gospel truth, but rather experiment and find your "sweet spots." Fortunately, once you tune your AdWords this generally takes just a few hours a month to double-check things.

Spot Checking Your Ads

Despite what Google says, I also recommend spot checking your ads periodically. Here's **method #1**. In AdWords, go to the *Tools* menu (under the wrench icon), and select *Ad Preview and Diagnosis*. Enter relevant search queries, set your location to a city in your target area, and "spot check" to verify that your ads are actually running. Here's a screenshot:

SEO Books   🔍   Location: Tulsa OK, United States   Language: English   Device: Desktop

✔ **Your ad is showing**

For the keyword [SEO books] (Books - Search Network > SEO Workbook - Amazon)

Preview of search results

Google   SEO Books   🔍

All   Books   News   Images   Shopping   More   Settings   Tools

Best Books on SEO? - SEO Fitness Workbook 2018 - amazon.com
[Ad] www.amazon.com/SEO-Book/2018 ▾
Master **Search Engine Optimization**. Step-by-step workbook. Videos & worksheets.
Video Links Included. · New for 2017 · Includes Worksheets.

This means that my ad for my *SEO Fitness Workbook* is showing for the search query *SEO books* with location set to Tulsa, Oklahoma. If you click on Device on the top menu, you can also toggle to mobile device and tablet, to see if your ad is showing on the mobile phone and/or tablet.

Unfortunately and bizarrely, sometimes the official AdWords tool will say your ad isn't running when it actually is. (*Reason #67 not to ever get in a Google self-driving car*). So for **method #2**, I also recommend opening up a Chrome browser in incognito mode and going to the SERPS.com location tool at **http://jmlinks.com/26z**. This tool is nice because it allows you to vary your city / location, and often it is more accurate than the Google tool. (It only shows you desktop results). Just do NOT click on your ad in the results, of course, as you'll get charged. If location doesn't matter to you, you can just check in the Chrome incognito browser directly.

TRUST BUT VERIFY

Between checking your impressions, that your SIS is > 85% and spot-checking, I reassure myself that my ads are running on Google. Note: if you're using Bing, Bing has a similar tool inside of its own ad interface, also located under the Tools Menu > Ad Preview. Here's a screenshot from Bing:

If your ads are not showing, then raise your bids of course. However, do your spot checking *before* making any bid changes, as it takes about 3-5 hours for Google to adjust to new bids. In fact, if you change your bids or your ad copy, and then attempt to preview your ads, they'll often go offline. So your process is first to log in to AdWords, check your SIS, spot check your ads using the Preview Tool, and then adjust your bids upwards or downwards.

Indeed, AdWords will sometimes say that your ads are "not running" because your bid is "too low," but when you spot check, you'll see your ads. You'll also see clicks, and performance – so, again, don't' believe everything that AdWords tells you.

Between spot-checking your ads and using the SIS score of > 85% and position of < 5, you can verify that your ads are running on desktop, on mobile phones, and on tablets as well as city-by-city if you are geotargeting. In this way, you are sure your ads are running and you can work in a more focused way on raising your click thru rate, lowering your bids as much as possible, and increasing your conversion rates once people land on your website.

What you're trying to do is to **tune your ads** by tightening the relationship between the Ad Group, the target keywords (and negative keywords), the ad copy, and the bid per click to get an SIS > 85%, a position of about 3, and the lowest possible CPC you can get away with, always with an eye to your conversions.

▶ Shoot Your Dogs and Let Your Winners Run

Next, click up or over to the Ads tab from within an Ad Group. This will show you the ads that are running in each Ad Group. I recommend running at least two, if not three, ads simultaneously. Compare the ads, especially their CTR or Click Thru Rate.

> **Run at least two ads per Ad Group.** Then "kill" (or at least pause) the lower performing ad as measured by CTR, and replace it with a new ad. Over time, you can thus optimize your ad performance by constantly "killing" the bad ads, and "running" the better ads. In fact, I find the best performance when I run multiple ads in an Ad Group and make sure that the different variations contain various permutations of the keyword targets.

I recommend that you "kill" your lower performing ads on at least a monthly basis, and rewrite them. Then, over time, compare your ads against each other, and run / select ads with the higher click-thru rate, and ultimately higher conversion rate. Google does this to some extent automatically, but by writing and re-writing your ads, you can improve your CTR.

Remember, however, to use the **Attract / Repel** strategy in writing your ads so as to not fall into the trap of writing ads with words like "free" or "cheap" that will get you a lot of clicks, but few valuable conversions. If at all possible, look for ads have both a good click thru rate and a good conversion rate.

Similarly, at the Ad Group level and Keyword level, look for high-performing keywords and Ad Groups. "Kill" your lower performing Ad Groups and/or Keywords, but first write / re-write your ads to make sure that the ad content isn't the problem.

Over time, you are looking to "shoot your dogs" and "let your winners run" by deleting low-performing keywords, Ad Groups, and even Campaigns and running / enhancing those that are performing. In the long term, performance is measured not by *clicks* or even *click thru rates*, but by *conversions* and money made!

≫ LEARN ABOUT A SPECIAL TYPE OF SEARCH AD: GOOGLE SHOPPING CAMPAIGNS

Before we leave the Search Network, we should note a special opportunity on Google, so-called **Google Shopping Campaigns** or as they used to be called **Product Listing Ads (PLAs)**. Google has, confusingly, named and renamed this ad type many times, so be aware that you may see it by various names. Among the more important is "Google Merchant Center." To see PLAs in action, try some product-centric searches on Google, for example:

> *running shoes*
>
> *red dresses*
>
> *wifi routers*

The PLAs appear at the top right, or center, of the screen and have a product image, product name, price, vendors, and some attributes such as "free shipping" or "star ratings". Here's a screenshot for the search query, *wifi routers*:

In order to get your products into Google Shopping, you need, first of all, to have either an e-Commerce store and/or a brick-and-mortar store that can generate a product inventory or feed. Here are your steps.

1. **Sign up for a Google Merchant Center account** at **http://jmlinks.com/24t**. Note: that link has a nice "Resource center" which includes help on how to set up your data feed.
2. **Populate your feed.** The most important elements are the *product title, description, image,* and *URL.* Be sure to write keyword-heavy titles and descriptions!
   a. Note: if your feed and URL are associated either with reviews on your own website and/or with reviews hosted on affiliated sites via *globally unique product identifiers*, Google will often pull the reviews and stars into your

ad as indicated above on the "Best Buy" router. (Read the help file at **http://jmlinks.com/24u**).

b. Note: sellers can also have seller ratings, which are ratings not of your products but of your company as a seller. These are often pulled from third-party sources such as Trustpilot, Zoorate, etc. (Read the help file at **http://jmlinks.com/24v**).

Once Google has accepted and validated your product feed, make sure to attach your Merchant Center account to your AdWords account. You can read the help file at **http://jmlinks.com/27a** for step-by-step instructions. You then set up a Shopping Campaign in AdWords as follows:

1. Click on white plus sign in the blue circle, and select *Shopping* as the Campaign type. (You'll need to have previously linked your AdWords account to a Merchant Center account)
2. Follow the steps concerning your merchant identifier and other miscellaneous attributes.
3. Use optional filters such as campaign priority or inventory to allow yourself to be able to control bids better.

Be sure to track your conversions, so that you can correlate your bids with your return on ad spend. It is very important to correlate bids with profit generated, as you can have a product that gets lots and lots of clicks via Google Shopping ads but either a) doesn't convert, or b) doesn't generate as much profit as your advertising spend. In many cases, you want to take out your flagship products and manage them very intensively by using inventory filters or specific feeds.

- For a nifty guide to Shopping / Product Listing Ads, visit **http://jmlinks.com/24w**.

▸▸ DELIVERABLE: SEARCH NETWORK WORKSHEET

The **DELIVERABLE** for this Chapter is a completed worksheet on the Search Network. This is a deep dive into your Keyword Patterns, Campaigns, Ad Groups, Ads, and

Keywords, so that you end up with a well-organized AdWords account, and -over time – are able to identify winning keywords and terminate non-winning keywords.

For the **worksheet**, go to **https://www.jm-seo.org/workbooks** (click on "AdWords Workbook 2018," enter the code 'adwords18' to register if you have not already done so), and click on the link to the "Search Network Worksheet."

SURVEY OFFER

CLAIM YOUR $5 SURVEY REBATE! HERE'S HOW –

- Visit **http://jmlinks.com/survey**.
- Take a short, simple survey about the book.
- Claim your rebate.

WE WILL THEN –

- Rebate you the $5 via Amazon eGift.

~ **$5 REBATE OFFER** ~

~ **LIMITED TO ONE PER CUSTOMER** ~

EXPIRES: 4/1/2018

SUBJECT TO CHANGE WITHOUT NOTICE

RESTRICTIONS APPLY

GOT QUESTIONS? CALL 800-298-4065

YOUR SAMPLE TEXT
YOUR SAMPLE TEXT YOUR SAMPLE TEXT YOUR SAMPLE TEXT

5

DISPLAY NETWORK

If you advertise on Google's **Display Network** or **GDN,** your ads don't appear on Google, but rather on blogs, news sites, videos, user forums, and other websites that participate in Google's network of content websites. For example, if your customers are reading *People Magazine, Chicago Tribune,* some esoteric blog on cats, or watching *Saturday Night Live*'s latest spoof of Donald Trump on *YouTube,* they can see your AdWords ads populated via the GDN. If they're checking email via Gmail or interacting with Apps on their phone, they can see ads as well, and so on and so forth. Through remarketing, you can "follow them around" as they browse the Internet. Sound too good to be true? Well, it *is* (and it *isn't*). The GDN can be a goldmine or a disaster, to your online advertising efforts.

Let's get started!

TODO LIST:

» Review the Basics of the GDN

» Set Up a Basic GDN Campaign

» Ad Group Organization on the Display Network

» Create Winning Ads on the Display Network

» Target Your Ad Group: Keywords

» Target Your Ad Group: Placements

» Target Your Ad Group: Remarketing

» Target Your Ad Group: Other Targeting Methods

» Target Your Ad Group: Apps

» Target Your Ad Group: Gmail

» Target Your Ad Group: Combining Methods

» Monitor Your Placements Exclude the Naughty

» Understand Bidding & Quality Score on the GDN

» Monitoring Your GDN Campaigns

»» Deliverable: Display Network Worksheet

» REVIEW THE BASICS OF THE GDN

As I explained in Chapter 1, Google advertising is really two distinct networks:

1. the **Search Network** (primarily Google but also search-driven sites like Yelp or Comcast), and
2. the **Display Network** (a network of sites such as YouTube and Gmail but also blogs, parked domains, apps, web portals and many nefarious sites). Note that the Display Network is referred to as the **AdSense Network** (**http://jmlinks.com/41e**) from the publisher site perspective.

Remember that you can see which network(s) you are running on by clicking into a Campaign, and then into the Settings tab on the left. Next, look for *Networks* in the center, and you should see "Search Network" for a Search campaign or "Display Network" for a Display Network Campaign. It is a best practice, of course, never to mix the Campaign types!

In this Chapter, of course, we're going to focus exclusively on Display Network campaigns.

VIDEO. Watch an (overly cheerful) video from Google on the Display Network at **http://jmlinks.com/27b**.

Search vs. Browse

Conceptually, the easiest way to grasp the difference between the two networks is to understand *browse* vs. *search*. Whereas in *search*, the target customer goes to Google and *pro-actively searches* for your product or service by keyword, in *browse*, he doesn't go to Google at all nor does he pro-actively enter in search keywords. Rather he's reading a blog or newspaper site, checking his email on Gmail or watching a YouTube video, and as he's browsing, he just *happens to see your ad* somewhere on the web page. *Search* is all about pro-active searching, and *browse* is about getting your ad "adjacent" to what the customer is actually paying attention to.

Two big points to remember about the Display Network are:

1. The GDN has **many poor quality sites** up to and including fraudulent sites, so ads on the GDN often generate many clicks but few conversions if you aren't careful.
2. Google is motivated to get you to advertise everywhere to get clicks, so official Google information on the GDN tends to be **overly optimistic**.

In general, the click thru rate (CTR) and the conversion rate on ads on the Display Network are many factors of ten lower than on the Search Network. This is because a) people are in "browse mode" on the GDN, so less likely to be primed to click or convert into a purchase and b) there is a lot of noise and even fraud on the GDN, so many clicks are purely frivolous and hence do not convert.

Google's Contradictions on the GDN

This is not the place for me to get on my soapbox about the contradictions among Google, its AdSense partners, and you the advertiser, but do take a moment to look at the incentive structure:

Google gets *paid by the click*, and is incentivized to maximize ad clicks on the network.

AdSense partners (i.e., websites and apps that participate in the Display Network) also get *paid by the click* (they share revenue with Google for each ad click), and are also incentivized to maximize ad clicks on the network.

You, as the advertiser, however, get *paid by the conversion* and are incentivized to minimize low-quality clicks (those that do not convert, or that yield low-value revenue).

Most problematically, Google has a conflict of interest in that it gets paid by clicks on the network yet is also charged with policing the network against fraud. We, as advertisers, are required to "trust Google" and its "partners" that they are not engaging in click fraud at the worst, or poor policing at best. To read a shocking account of the problem visit **http://jmlinks.com/25f**, and be sure to read the comments / discussion.

To be fair, it's not just Google's AdSense ad network that operates under a cloud of suspicion; it's all the ad networks, but Google's is probably the largest. It's not surprising, therefore, that after the 2017 Presidential Election when both Google and Facebook were criticized for fake news schemes (which largely made money via AdSense), that the *New York Times* accused the Silicon Valley giants of dragging their feet (**http://jmlinks.com/24b**).

Why Advertise on the Display Network?

If the GDN is so problematic, why advertise on it? Here are a few important reasons:

- **Browse over search**. While the Search Network is fantastic if, and only if, people are pro-actively searching for keywords that relate to your product or service, the GDN can get you in front of potential customers across a plethora of websites (adjacent to their interests), thereby getting you in front of customers who might not be pro-actively searching for a product or service like yours.
- **Niche Targeting**. The GDN can identify blogs and other websites in an industry niche, and place your ad precisely on these niche venues. In this way, a company that sells high-end biking supplies can "build its brand" by advertising specifically on high-value cyclist websites on a recurring basis.
- **Repeating your message**. For items with long sales cycles and high values, like Caribbean cruises or life insurance, the GDN allows an advertiser to reach potential customers not just at the moment of search but to "follow them" around the Internet over the days, weeks, or even months that they toy with a big purchase decision.
- **Brand and Awareness Building**. By combining the GDN with the Search Network, you can constantly remind your target audience of your company and

brand. Brand-building – the constant repetition of a company's message – is now available to even small, nichey companies via the GDN.

The GDN is a tool that has its uses. But if you choose to advertise on the GDN, just be aware of its contradictions and commit to regularly monitoring your placements and performance for fraud and low-value placements.

How the Display Network Works

At its simplest level, the Display Network works as follows:

- **Publishers** with websites or apps join AdSense (**http://jmlinks.com/24a**) and become part of Google's **Display Network**. They agree to allow Google to place ads on their websites and/or apps.
- **Advertisers** set up Display Network campaigns in AdWords and tell Google where to place their ads via targeting methods such as *keywords, placements,* or *remarketing* (discussed in detail, below).
- As **users** browse websites and apps, Google places ads on the websites or apps (called "placements" in GDN lingo). Users see these ads as they browse websites, apps, YouTube, and Gmail.
- Advertisers *compete* to get their ads on placements (websites and/or apps) in the Google Display Network by bidding per click and/or by impression.
- When a **user clicks on an ad**, Google makes money off the click and splits this with the publisher of the website and/or app.
- The **user** then leaves the website, and **lands** on the **advertiser landing page**, where he either converts or doesn't.

Publishers get paid by the click. Advertisers compete in the auction by the click. Google makes money, the publishers make money, and you as the advertiser spend money to get traffic to your website. If you've done your homework, you can get high-quality traffic to your website that actually converts and makes you money. If you haven't done your homework, you'll just spend money on frivolous placements and even fake / bot clicks.

VIDEO. Watch a video from Google on how to advertise on the Google Display Network at **http://jmlinks.com/26f**.

» SET UP A BASIC GDN CAMPAIGN

In order to understand how the GDN works, you'll need a basic GDN campaign if you don't have one running already. Here's how. If you already have a GDN Campaign, you can skip this section.

First, log in to your AdWords account, and click into Campaigns, and then click the blue circle to start creating a new Campaign. Select Display Network. Here's a screenshot:

Next, select a subtype – *Sales, Leads, Website traffic, Product and brand consideration,* or *brand awareness and reach.* Most of us want **website traffic**, so that is the most common subtype. Then choose either Standard display campaign or Gmail (if you want ads to show on Gmail, Google's email system). (*We'll focus on Standard display campaigns from here forward*). Give your Campaign a name (*I recommend naming it with the suffix – GDN so you know it's a GDN Campaign*), select the Geotarget (e.g., Stamford, Connecticut, or 25 miles from Stamford, CT, for example). Select a Bidding strategy such as Manual CPC and a budget.

Click Additional Settings in blue to open up the additional settings. Here you can set up very specific things, and I recommend you use **frequency capping** so that a person does not see your ad over and over and over and over again. A good limit is three times per day per Campaign. Here's a screenshot:

Frequency capping	Set a limit to how many times your ads appear to the same user on the Display Network ⑦
	◯ No limit on viewable impressions
	◉ Apply limit on viewable impressions

Number of impressions	Frequency	Level
3	per day ▾	this campaign

Next, create and name at least one Ad Group, and give it a budget and bids. Unfortunately, the first set up is a supremely annoying set of steps. But once you've gotten to the Ad Group, you can skip to the bottom and click "Create Campaign." In fact, I recommend you do so (rather than set up everything at once as Google recommends), as it is easier to manage everything once you have the "shell" of at least one Campaign and one Ad Group. Ignore the warning messages, and then once you've gotten a Campaign created, **pause** it so you don't waste any money.

It's very important to <u>pause your Campaign</u> until you are 100% ready as Google has a new "feature" that will run your ads with no targeting at all, just to make Google money. The whole set up process from scratch is extremely annoying and difficult as they throw too many questions at you too quickly. So just set up a Campaign with an Ad Group that is set to run on the GDN, and pause it. Now, you're ready to dig into your first Campaign.

Two Key Settings: just as on the Search Network you can geotarget your ads, and opt in or opt out of desktop, mobile, and/or tablet traffic by adjusting your settings on the Campaign Settings tab. Therefore:

1. Select a **geotarget** for your campaign. For example, if you are a hair salon in Stamford, CT, then choose a radius of 10 miles from your salon. This means, for example, that someone browsing a website in the GDN or watching a YouTube video who is also within 10 miles of your shop is eligible to see your ad, while someone outside of 10 miles is not.

2. Select your **device targeting** of phones, tablets, and/or desktop. Make at least an educated guess as to which platform(s) will convert best for you, and set the device targeting accordingly.

≫ AD GROUP ORGANIZATION ON THE DISPLAY NETWORK

We will get to targeting settings in a moment, but first, let's review the basics of how to organize your Ad Groups on the GDN. First and foremost, your Ad Groups should reflect your product / service lines or your core keywords from your search campaign. For example, for Jason's Cat Emporium, we might have the following three Ad Groups:

Cat Boarding targeting people who need to board their cat for vacation.

Cat Grooming targeting people who want to get their cat professionally groomed.

Cat Toys targeting people who want to buy luxury toys for their cat.

Keywords are very loose on the Display Network, so think of these as thematically connected one to each Ad Group. Each group is more a way to help you organize your ads thematically than a tight match between keyword and ad as on the Search Network.

Secondarily, targeting (as we shall discuss in a moment) "lives" at the Ad Group level on a Display Campaign (vs. at the Campaign level in a Search Campaign), so if you want to target in different ways you would do best not to mix and match targeting methods in one single group. For example, you might have an Ad Group that uses *remarketing* (re-showing your ads to people who have visited your website), another one that uses *keyword targeting*, and still another that targets *Gmail* only. Even if each were to be promoting your "cat boarding" service line, they should have their own unique Ad Group in your GDN campaign.

Your **TODO** here is to outline your Ad Groups, starting with your product / service lines (or core keywords) and splitting them, if necessary, if you will be using different targeting methods. (You might want to read the whole Chapter first, so you understand targeting options if you're not sure.)

>> CREATE WINNING ADS ON THE GDN

Now let's dive into how to create ads for the GDN. While ads on the Search Network (e.g., Google) are limited to text, ads on the Display Network can be images as well as text. Indeed, they can even be interactive and engaging to the mouse!

Inside one of your Ad Groups, click on the blue button, and you'll see two options:

Upload display ads. This option allows you to upload your own graphics. It's useful if you are a larger company and want to control the look and feel of your ads tightly. Click through and then click on the blue "Supported sizes and formats" to learn the specifications. You should **upload all available formats**, as you do not know which format will match which placement on the network. In addition, you should create at least the **text version** of the Responsive ad type as some placements in the network only allow text ads.

Responsive Ad (recommended option) – this is a combination of both graphic and text ads and is the most common and most useful option. When you click on this, then

- Choose *create ad* (to scan your website), and then *responsive ad*. Similar to an ad on the Search network, enter your Short headline, Long headline, Description, Business Name, and Final URL.
- For images, you can either upload your own images, use Google's free library, or "scan" your website to pull images directly from your landing page.

Think Billboard Advertising.

While ads on the Search Network (i.e., Google itself) are more like ads in the old-fashioned yellow pages, where a user is pro-actively searching for a service (like a plumber or a roofer), very likely to look at ads, and primed to buy after the click, ads on the Display Network are more like billboards on the side of a highway. Users are zipping along, on their way to other destinations, and your job is to attract the attention of relevant customers and get them to shift from "what they're doing" to "hey, I want to visit that website."

- For fun, browse funny billboards and ponder how they make you take notice at **http://jmlinks.com/27c**. Now, return to your own ads and brainstorm how to make them visually "pop" as users are browsing sites on the Internet.

In terms of the technical ad production, AdWords' "scan website" feature makes it very easy to quickly create ads for all available formats on the Display Network. Just click "scan website" and follow the step-by-step instructions. Google does a great job of pulling graphics from your website and giving you options to configure your ads. Here's a screenshot:

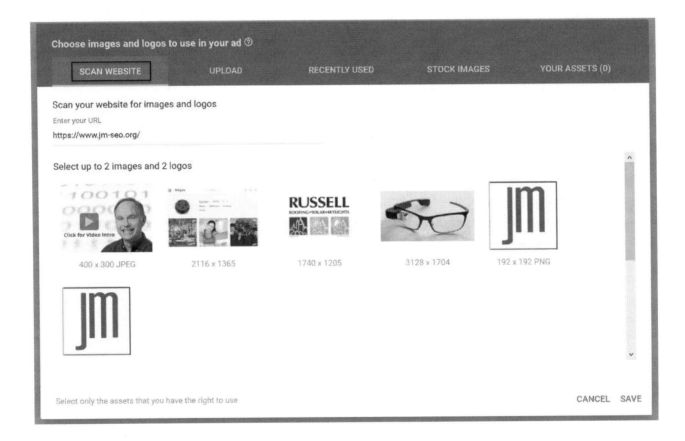

Once your ad is created, you can preview it and even email the preview to other people on your team.

Attract / Repel Ad Copy

Similar to the Search Network, remember that your best ad strategy is **attract / repel**. You don't want zillions of clicks but rather clicks from highly qualified buyers who ultimately convert to sales. Accordingly, think of ads that will "attract" your best customers but "repel" those who are not likely to buy, or likely to spend just a little money. Don't be afraid to scare off cheap people, or persons who are unlikely actually to buy your product or service. A good ad on the Display Network –

- is *available in all image sizes*, including the text only option;
- clearly conveys your *business value proposition*, including what is unique and attractive about your product or service;
- contains a *call to action* such as "free download" or "call for consultation"; and
- *attracts* your target customers while *repelling* those who might click but not convert.

Populate at least one Ad Group with all relevant ad formats with clever "attract / repel" ads, and you're ready to dive into how to **target** or **trigger** your ads, which is where the complexity and power of the Display Network truly lies.

» TARGET YOUR AD GROUP: KEYWORDS

Next, let's talk about ad **targets**, which is how you tell Google to **trigger** your ad to be displayed on the GDN. (Like Google, I will use *target* and *trigger* interchangeably to mean the same thing: how you communicate to Google as to when to show your ad). Just as on the Search Network, ads are shown based on your *bid per click* in the ad auction (you have to outbid your competition to run your ad, based on what you're willing to pay per click), plus your *Quality Score* (the higher the click thru rate, the more relevant the ad, and the more relevant your landing page, the more likely your ad is to run), plus your *trigger* or *target*. On the Search Network, the only trigger is the *keyword*; on the Google Display Network, it's more complicated.

*Let's go through each trigger one-by-one, starting with **keywords**.*

Keywords as a trigger mechanism exist in both the Search Network and the Display Network but function in very different ways.

Keyword matching is **tight** on the Search Network. (*Exact, phrase, modified broad, and broad*).

Keyword matching is **loosey-goosey** on the Display Network!

Google doesn't explain this clearly, but here's what I mean. On the Search Network, the user pro-actively types keywords into Google, such as *cat boarding, cat kennel,* or *cat grooming* (or keywords such as *dog boarding, iguana boarding,* or *exotic bird grooming*). Google knows user intent because after all, a person who types in *dog boarding* isn't looking for *iguana boarding* and a person who types in *cat grooming* isn't looking for an *exotic bird hotel*! Some keywords are problematic (e.g., *cheap cat boarding, pet boarding*), but we as advertisers manage those through negative keywords and through writing attract / repel ad copy.

KEYWORD MATCHING IS LOOSEY-GOOSEY ON THE GDN

Not so on the Display Network. A user doesn't type anything in when he visits the Chicago Tribune's article on *Cats at the Westminster Kennel club dog show? Sort of, in a first* (**http://jmlinks.com/24c**), or when he's reading a Gmail from his Aunt Nancy on best recipes for Chicken Pot Pies for their weekend family reunion in Nebraska, or when he's on an App for how to de-stress. Google can spider the content and take a guess at what's important, but is the *Chicago Tribune* article more about cats or about dogs? Is the user a cat lover or a dog lover, or just a Chicago resident? As for the Gmail on Aunt Nancy and Chicken pot pies, is it about chicken, about Nebraska, about a family reunion, or about pot? As for apps, they're also all over the place.

Accordingly, keyword matching between the desires of the advertiser and the intent / interests of the user is loosey-goosey on the GDN!

The reality is that, despite Google's façade as an "all-knowing" tech company, on the Google Display Network, it simply makes its best guess at what it calls "contextual targeting" (**http://jmlinks.com/24d**), meaning it attempts to match the content of the article on the Web, video on YouTube, email on Gmail, or app, with the keywords entered by advertisers.

In short, the keywords you enter as triggers for a Display Network Campaign only match the keywords of the article in what I call a "loosey goosey" fashion, meaning not very much and certainly not with the laser precision available on the Search Network. Accordingly, you want to think of a GDN Campaign as attempting to reach people who are *browsing* on themes and topics related to your products in a very broad way.

Accordingly, while on the Search Network, I recommend you think in a very focused and detailed way about your keywords, on the Display Network, I recommend you relax and think more broadly about keywords, including ones adjacent to your product or service area. It's loosey-goosey!

Input Your Keywords

An easy way to get started on the GDN is to copy the structure of your search campaigns. So take a Campaign that is running on the Search Network, and then duplicate its Ad Groups on the GDN. If you don't have your keyword list handy, you can export your keywords from a Search Network. Just click into an Ad Group, click on Keywords on the left, and then find the downward arrow on the top right. Here's a screenshot:

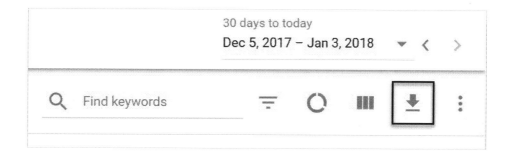

Export them into a CSV or Excel file, and remove all the "+" signs, "quote" marks or brackets as well as any duplicates. You just want the keywords with no markers for the Display Network.

With your keyword list in hand, click over to your Display Network Campaign, and then the matching Ad Group.

Next, at the Ad Group level, click on the Display Network tab, and then click on the Display Keywords tab. Here's a screenshot:

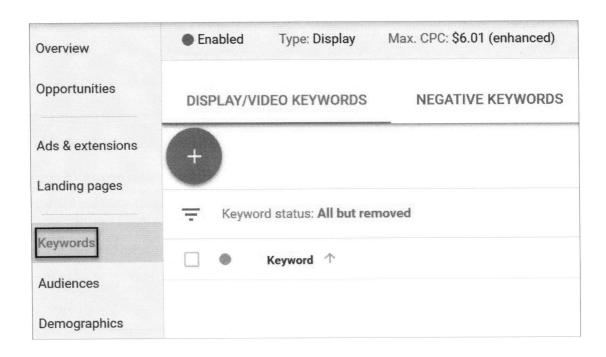

Click the blue circle, click "Add display keywords," and copy/paste in your keywords. The default setting at the bottom is "Audience," which means Google will do its best to match your keywords to the user profile as people are browsing the network. If you want to be tighter, matching only web pages that contain these keywords select "Content."

Do not mix targeting methods! You'll see other targeting methods on the left such as Audiences, Demographics, Topics, etc., but despite their availability, you'll have an easier time managing things if you just use one, and only one, targeting method per Ad Group. In fact, I recommend you name your GDN Ad Groups based on their targeting method such as *Cat boarding: keywords* or *Cat boarding: placements,* so you know which Ad Group is using which targeting method.

❯❯ TARGET YOUR AD GROUP: PLACEMENTS

While most of us will use the Keyword targeting method, there are other targeting methods. Next up is the "Placement" methodology. Let's say that you really like specific websites in your industry, or you'd like to pre-select the websites onto which Google will put your ads. You can be much more in control by choosing *placements.*

At the Ad Group level, click *Placements* on the left. Click the blue circle and then click Add Placements. Here's a screenshot:

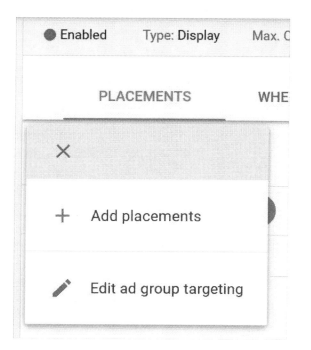

Here's where it gets a little tricky. If you know the placements you want to run on and you are sure that they are in the Google Display Network, then you can add them as URLs (domains). For example, both CNN.com and Entrepreneur.com run Google ads, so you can click *Enter multiple placements* at the bottom and then add them. Here's a screenshot:

If you're not sure whether a placement is (or is not) in the Google Display Network, you can do some research. (**Note**: even though you can enter any website domain into *Placements*, that doesn't mean your ads will show on that website. *JM-SEO.org* or *Facebook.com*, for example, can be entered but because neither site participates in AdSense, these are moot entries).

Returning to your process of identifying possible placements, you want to build a placement list. The trick here is NOT to add website domains as you find them, but rather use the built-in tool to discover them and build a list on a Notepad or Excel spreadsheet outside of AdWords first.

Here are the steps.

First, at the Ad Group level, click on *Placements* on the left. Click the blue circle and then *Add placements*. Second, where it says in gray *Search by word, phrase, URL, or video ID*, enter a relevant keyword such as *cat boarding*. Here's a screenshot:

PLACEMENTS WHERE ADS SHOWED EXCLUSIONS

◉ Targeting (recommended)
Narrow the reach of your ad group to specific audiences, and get reports. You'll have the option to ad

○ Observation ⑦
Get reports on additional items without narrowing the reach of your ad group. You'll have the option

cat boarding	⊗	None selected
Websites (1K+)	>	Your ad can ap
YouTube channels (308)	>	match your oth
YouTube videos (1K+)	>	targeting.
Apps (182)	>	
App categories	>	

Third, click on Websites and AdWords will open up a list of "relevant" websites. Here's a screenshot:

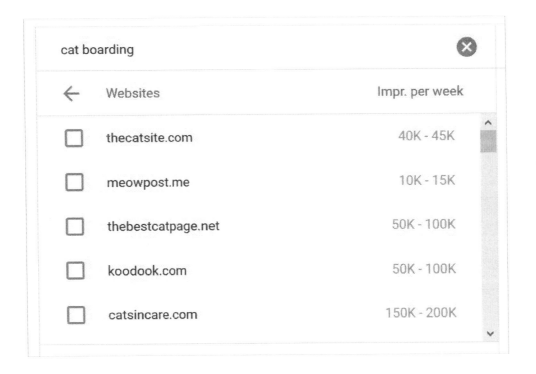

Fourth, do not add them at this time! Rather, copy paste the URL such as *thecatsite.com*, or *meowpost.me* into a new tab on your website. Check out the website and decide if you think it is relevant to your target customer. If so, add it to your Notepad or Excel. If not, do not add it. In this way, you can build up a list of high volume, relevant websites on which to run your ads and avoid the problem of nefarious sites or poor matches.

Note you can also use a tool called the **Display Planner** to identify possible placements. It is only available in the old interface, however. To access it, go to **http://jmlinks.com/41r**, but remember you may have to toggle back to the old AdWords interface. Google has not been clear on whether this tool is being discontinued or has not yet made it into the new AdWords interface.

Once you have a list of your domains (e.g., *thecatsite.com, catsincare.com*), then copy / paste this list from your Notepad or Excel by clicking *Enter multiple placements*. Finally, note (as I will explain below) that you can **combine** placements and keywords as a targeting method. For example, you could then run on *thecatsite.com* PLUS keyword = *boarding* to show ONLY on articles on the site that talked about *boarding*, or you could run on *CNN.com* and ONLY on articles on the site that talked about *marketing* if you were selling marketing services, for example. In this way, you can vastly tighten the focus of a Display Network Ad Group.

►► TARGET YOUR AD GROUP: REMARKETING

You've probably had the experience of visiting a website, such as Progressive.com or Zappos.com, clicking around; perhaps even adding a product or two to your shopping cart, and then, the next thing you know, you start seeing **recurring ads** for that vendor over and over and over and over and over again as you browse other sites on the Internet such as YouTube, Chicago Tribune, People Magazine, etc. What's going on?

It's called **remarketing**, and it's the next type of trigger available on the GDN. As you first visit sites on the Internet, such as Progressive.com or ChicagoTribune.com, for example, each website places a cookie or "tag" on your browser, and then through the magic of Google AdWords remarketing, you can be shown "relevant" ads by that vendor as you browse other sites that participate in Google's Display Network.

> **Remarketing** allows you a "second chance" to convert a customer by allowing you to show / reshow ads to him as he surfs other websites on the Internet after first visiting your website. That's why it's called **RE**marketing.

Remarketing vs. Retargeting: Conceptually Different

Remarketing is a little different than *retargeting*, and Google participates in the former as well as the latter. *Retargeting* is when you reach people who have not first visited your website but who are matched as "similar" to your target customers by a third party service, whether that be Google or true third party retargeting vendors such as AdRoll (**https://adroll.com**). Indeed, you can use remarketing and retargeting on Facebook as well (Facebook's system is probably #2 to Google's for remarketing / retargeting).

Let's return to Google AdWords, and think of it this way:

> *Remarketing* is reaching people who have touched your website at least once.

> *Retargeting* is reaching "similar audiences" who have not yet touched your website for the first time.

Unfortunately, the blogosphere uses the two terms interchangeably, but they are conceptually distinct.

Remarket High-Value Products or Services

Remarketing works best for a high-value product or service that has a long sales cycle. An example would be a Caribbean cruise. It's expensive and a big commitment to take your family on a Caribbean cruise, so you'll probably do some research, check out a few of the big vendors such as Disney Cruise Lines, Carnival Cruise Lines, and Norwegian Cruise Lines and discuss the options and expenses with your spouse and family. It's expensive, and it has a long cycle from interest to purchase!

REMARKETING WORKS BEST

FOR HIGH-VALUE PRODUCTS

Cruise line marketing is an excellent choice for remarketing, because you might first search "Caribbean cruises" on Google (Search Network), visit a few sites like Disney Cruises or Carnival Cruises, and then go watch videos on YouTube about Jamaica, Cuba, Barbados and other destinations (Display Network). You might research snorkeling, things to do in Kingston, Jamaica, etc., and only then return to vendor sites to select your cruise line. There's a lot of back and forth, many websites that get visited, a long time between interest and purchase, and a high-value purchase.

This makes it ideal for remarketing.

By using remarketing, Carnival Cruise Line can transform that *first* visit you make to their website into a *continuous remarketing effort* as you visit site after site after site after site in the Google Display Network. Remarketing extends that opportunity for Carnival Cruise Lines to sell to you from the short-time interaction on their website to the long-time interaction as you browse many sites as you research every aspect of planning your perfect family vacation to the Caribbean.

Note: remarketing is not available in sensitive categories such as healthcare, pharmaceuticals, gun purchases, etc. If your website category is not eligible, you're remarketing code will be invalidated after installation. And **note**: remarketing is generally not effective for *low-value products* as the cost per click can be quite expensive.

Setting up Remarketing

To enable remarketing, you have to install a little Google Javascript tracking code on your website. Yes, you, too, can participate in Google's massive invasion of our privacy across the Internet by participating in remarketing and installing the tracking code! (If you'd like to see what Google thinks your personal preferences are, make sure you're signed into your Gmail or Google account, and visit **http://jmlinks.com/24q**; if you'd like to see what Google knows about the websites you've visited, go to **http://jmlinks.com/24r**. The point is that *remarketing* is how Google, in cooperation with sites on the Display Network and advertisers, uses what it knows about you (and others) to show you relevant ads as you visit sites in the GDN).

Create a Remarketing List

In order to use remarketing, you have to create a remarketing list. The most common way to do this is to "tag" everyone who visits your website. So your first step is to set up and enable the AdWords remarketing tag on your website. Here's how.

First, log in to AdWords and click on the tools menu at the top. Select Audience manager. Here's a screenshot:

Next, click *Audience sources* and follow the steps there. The easiest way to do it is to enable Google Analytics via Google Tag Manager and cross-link AdWords to Google Tag Manager / Analytics. You can read the step-by-step instructions on Google at **http://jmlinks.com/39y** as well as how to link Google Analytics and AdWords at **http://jmlinks.com/39z**. I recommend you use the new Google Tag Manager (**http://jmlinks.com/41b**) and follow the instructions at **http://jmlinks.com/41a**. It's a little complicated, so you may need to bring you're your resident computer nerd. Or click the *Question Mark* icon on the top right and reach out to AdWords technical support by phone. They'll lead you through it.

Note that you can have a list of everyone who has hit your website as well as smaller lists such as people who did not convert, or people who hit the *cat boarding* landing page vs. the *cat toys* landing page. It can be very focused.

Using Tag Assistant to Verify Your Installation

Google has, unfortunately, done a very bad job of explaining how to set up and install the remarketing tag. It can be pretty confusing! Like Google Analytics, the remarketing tag is a little Javascript code that you MUST get installed on each and every page of your website.

Fortunately, as you play around with the required code in Google AdWords, Google Analytics, and Google Tag Manager, there is a Chrome plugin that will test your remarketing code installation. It's called **Tag Assistant** by Google (**http://jmlinks.com/24h**). Install it, visit your website, and then at the top right of your browser, you can test your installation. Here's a screenshot of Tag Assistant confirming that the remarketing tag is activated on JasonMcDonald.org:

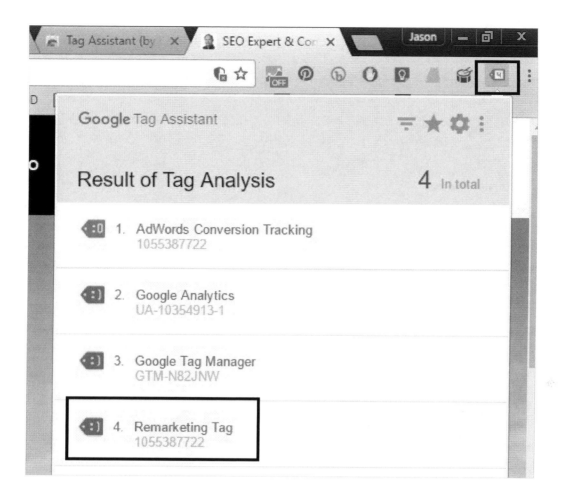

You can also use Tag Assistant on other websites (e.g., competitors) to see if they are using remarketing.

Once you've set up an audience, give it a few weeks and then check the audience in AdWords to verify that there are "people" in it. Login to AdWords, click on the *Tools Menu > Audience Manager*. You should then see your list, and it should have numeric values for the *Size:Display* column. Here's a screenshot:

Audience lists

+		Enabled audiences ▾
☐	**Audience name** ↑	Size: Display
In-use		
☐	All visitors People who visited pages that contain your remarketing tags	990

If you show a positive, growing number to your list, then it's working. You are now "tagging" people as they visit your website, and you can remarket (i.e., show your ads to them), wherever they are on the Display Network.

With your list in hand, return to the Ad Group that you want to target using remarketing. Click into the Ad Group, and then click *Audiences*. Click the blue circle, and then under *Targeting* click *Remarketing*. Find your list and select it. Voila! Your ads will now show to someone who is "on" the list anywhere that they are on the GDN. Be aware that they don't necessarily realize that they've been "remarketed to." Many people are mystified at how ads "follow them" around the Internet, and this is how. If you want to be more aggressive, you can use *retargeting*, by selecting *Similar audiences*, for example. AdWords will attempt to match "your list" to "their lists." However, I do not generally recommend this setting as it isn't usually a very good match.

To read the official Google help file on remarketing, visit **http://jmlinks.com/41c**.

RLSA Ads

In a special twist, there are even what are called "Remarketing Lists for Search" or RLSA ads. In this way, you "remarket" to people who are searching Google. That is, someone who is "on" your list can be "remarketed to" when he or she returns to Google and does a search. An example of this would be when someone searches for a vacation, hits the Disney.com website (and gets "tagged" for remarketing), and then returns to Google to search for things such as airline tickets, hotels, travel information about Anaheim or

Orlando, etc. The ads on Google Search are thus triggered not directly by the search keywords but rather by the remarketing list. It's a hybrid! Read about RLSA at **http://jmlinks.com/41d**.

Ad Groups and Remarketing Lists

Remember this is a targeting method, only, and that the targeting method or trigger "lives" at the Ad Group level in AdWords. Accordingly, the best practice is to match a targeting method to an Ad Group. For example, you might set up:

> Persons who clicked the Jamaica cruise page > Jamaica targeting group > Ads on Jamaica cruises.

> Persons who clicked the Cabo San Lucas cruise page > Cabo San Lucas targeting group > Ads on Cabo San Lucas cruises.

And remember, at the end of the day, they'll see the ads NOT on your website but on other sites such as People.com, ChicagoTribune.com, YouTube, Gmail, and other participating sites in the Display Network.

As you create your ads, upload highly relevant text and image ads, or use the Responsive Ad tool to create a series of ads. As the person browses sites on the Internet, then she'll see your ads again and again (until she clicks and converts).

So the process is:

> **Remarketing List** (e.g., *all website visitors, visitors to the cat boarding page who did not convert, visitors to the cat grooming page who did not convert*, etc.) > **targeting method** in AdWords > **show ads** to these people as they browse various sites on the Internet that participate in the Google Display Network.

The beauty of remarketing is that you know these people are highly qualified (*why else would they have visited your website?*), and you don't have to worry about placements on the GDN – Google will automatically follow them around the Internet! Remarketing as a targeting method is less vulnerable to nefarious or fraudulent sites, which is another plus. Indeed, the sky's the limit, and you can even create *dynamic remarketing ads,* showing people very specific ads relating to the very specific products or services that they have visited (but not purchased) on your website. To watch a Google video on dynamic remarketing ads, visit **http://jmlinks.com/24m**.

Setting a Frequency Cap

Because people get annoyed at seeing an ad over and over and over again, one tip is to set a "frequency cap" so that they might see your ad just two or three times. To do this, go to the Campaign level, click on *Settings* on the left, and then *Additional Settings* in the middle. Set a limit such as three per day. This means that no individual will see your ads more than three times in one day, which helps reduce the annoyance factor. Here's a screenshot:

Frequency capping	Set a limit to how many times your ads appear to the same user on the Display Network ⑦		∧
	○ No limit on viewable impressions		
	◉ Apply limit on viewable impressions		
	Number of impressions	Frequency	Level
	3	per day ▾	this campaign ▾
			CANCEL SAVE

In fact, setting a frequency cap is a good idea across the all your Display Network campaigns as it also helps fight click fraud, so I recommend you do this for every GDN campaign.

Note, of course, that you pay by click so, at some level, you don't need to be too concerned about showing your remarketing ads pretty frequently. For this reason, I recommend pretty high-frequency caps like three times a day or ten times a week.

Bids on Remarketing

Finally, whatever type of remarketing / retargeting you may decide to do, be aware that you will generally have to bid pretty high to get your ads to run because many, many advertisers are using remarketing and you are competing against a very large universe to get your remarketing ads to run. Just as on the Search Network, bids on the Display

Network are set at the Ad Group level. Often times, however, focused ads on the Google Search Network are, ironically, often cheaper than remarketing ads because of the intense competition for remarketing by big brands.

▶▶ TARGET YOUR AD GROUP: OTHER TARGETING METHODS

There are a few other targeting methods that are worth mentioning. We've looked at the big three – keywords, placements, and remarketing. Most advertisers need not go beyond these big three. However, there are other targeting methods.

Here is a summary:

Affinity. Google has categorized people based on their long-term interests, such as banking and finance, food & dining, media & entertainment, etc. You can drill down even farther such as *Sports & Fitness > Sports fans* to identify people who love to "watch" sports vs. "do" sports, for example.

Intent. Here, Google has categorized people by snooping into how they are searching and browsing to complete an action (usually to buy something). Drilling down here to *In-market audiences*, for example, means people who are "in the market" to buy something like a car or baby products.

Demographics. Google attempts to identify people by age group, and you can target them.

Topics. These are people who are searching or browsing more general topics such as Arts & Entertainment, Business & Industrial, etc. It's similar to *affinity* but more short term.

In my experience, none of these are very good except for **in-market audiences**. If there is an in-market audience that specifically matches your target customer (e.g., business loans, credit cards or employment, accounting & finance jobs, or dating services), it can be a pretty good choice. (This makes sense because Google knows the most about us based on what we search for (a.k.a., "intent"), which tracks pretty closely with being "in the market" for such-and-such product or service). Regardless, experiment, track your conversions, and you may find something that works for you. What works for one advertiser / product / service will not work for another and vice-versa, so deploy and test, deploy and test, rinse and repeat, etc.!

>> TARGET YOUR AD GROUP: APPS

One novel feature of the Display Network is **in-app ads**. You can advertise to people who are using apps that participate in the GDN. To show ads to people using apps, create a new Campaign and select Universal App on the far right. This campaign type is available only on the GDN and is best used if you have an app of your own that you are promoting. You can also conceivably advertise a website via app advertising, but this will show up as a placement in a Display Network campaign and be marked "Mobile App" in the Placements tab.

>> TARGET YOUR AD GROUP: GMAIL

Gmail is Google's free email service and is used by millions of people. You can target Gmail as a "placement" on the Google Display Network and get your ads to show on Gmail. It's one of the better opportunities, along with YouTube, that are Google-owned and Google-operated and so less prone to fraud and problems than the wider Google network.

> **VIDEO.** Watch a video from Google on how to advertise on Gmail at **http://jmlinks.com/27d**.

If you think that customers will be emailing back and forth with friends, families, and colleagues on a topic that's related to your business, it's worth trying out ads on Gmail. A cruise / family vacation, for example, will often generate a lot of emails and is a good candidate for Gmail ads. Google has an excellent step-by-step help file on how to set up ads on Gmail at **http://jmlinks.com/25g**.

>> TARGET YOUR AD GROUP: COMBINING METHODS

Remember that you can mix and match features in AdWords. So, for example, you could have an Ad Group using remarketing for people who are interested in Caribbean cruises who live in Chicago, by having a Campaign that is geotargeted at people who live in Chicago and have an in-market audience of cruises, or people who are using their mobile phones to target consumers who skew young.

It's a good idea to sit down with a spreadsheet and draft out your parameters, as for example:

Search. People who are searching for Caribbean cruises using keywords like "Caribbean cruises" or "Cruises to Jamaica."

Remarketing. People who landed on your website, but did not convert, so you show / reshow them your ads for a Jamaica Cruise as they visit sites like Chicago Tribune, YouTube, People Magazine, etc.

Retargeting. Let Google think for you, and find people similar to your remarketing list, and show them ads on the Display Network.

Mobile. Show specific ads to people using their phones vs. their desktop computers.

Geotarget. Show ads to people in specific areas (e.g., Chicago vs. Miami).

Schedule. Show ads during specific days, or times of the day.

Etc.

You can, in summary, mix and match features in AdWords – the sky's the limit!

As for **targeting methods**, you can also mix and match targeting methods on the GDN, but I would generally advise against it. I recommend you think of scenarios, first, and targeting methods, second. For example, for a cruise line, moving down from the "most likely" to convert to the "least likely," you'd have:

Best choices -

Search. People pro-actively searching for Caribbean cruises. (Best choice: Google Search Network, targeting method: **keywords**).

Search: People pro-actively searching adjacent searches (e.g., "Things to do in Jamaica) who have hit your website but did not convert. (Best choice: Google Search Network, targeting method: **RLSA**).

Then second best choice -

Browse. People who have landed on your website, but did not convert. (Best choice: Google Display Network, targeting method: **remarketing**).

Then third level choices -

Browse. People who are browsing sites on the Caribbean, on cruises, even on Jamaica. (Best choice: Google Display Network, targeting method: **placements**).

Browse. People who are browsing sites on the Caribbean, on cruises, even on Jamaica. (Best choice: Google Display Network, targeting method: **keywords**).

Browse. People who are browsing sites on the Caribbean, on cruises, even on Jamaica. (Best choice: Google Display Network, targeting method: **in-market audiences**).

Browse. People who are browsing sites on the Caribbean, on cruises, even on Jamaica. (Best choice: Google Display Network, targeting method: **similar to remarketing lists)**

Browse. People who are browsing sites on the Caribbean, on cruises, even on Jamaica. (Best choice: Google Display Network, targeting method: **affinity**).

Remember, you can see your choice options by going to a **Display Network Campaign > Ad Group**, scrolling along the left column. AdWords doesn't make it easy to see which ones are "on" and which ones are "off," so I recommend naming your Ad Groups to clearly mark their targeting method such as naming your GDN Ad Groups something like:

Cat boarding: keywords

Cat boarding: remarketing

Cat boarding: in-market audience

etc.

Combining Targeting Methods

With the exclusion of the Search Network, you can combine targeting methods. Generally, I would NOT recommend that you do this. It's easier to manage if you have ONE Ad Group have ONE targeting method, as in ONE Ad Group that uses keywords and ONE Ad Group that uses remarketing. Technically speaking, however, you can combine them into "and" statements, as in "OK Google, show my ad to a remarketing customer who you also think is relevant because the keyword is 'Jamaica vacation,'" but because targeting is loosey-goosey on the GDN, I wouldn't recommend overthinking this.

One example where you might want to combine methods is PLACEMENTS and KEYWORDS. So, you might want people who are on CNN.com AND using keywords "Caribbean cruise," because CNN.com is a huge site with many irrelevant areas. You can read a detailed explanation on combining targeting methods at **http://jmlinks.com/24n**. Again, for most of us, I would do, at most, the Search Network and then perhaps remarketing and/or placement targeting and leave it at that. In the New Interface, these are now marked as "Targeting" and "Observation," the former being a "trigger" and the latter just being a "reporting point."

Don't overthink it. The GDN is loosey-goosey, so be prepared to cast a wide net!

» UNDERSTAND BIDDING & QUALITY SCORE ON THE GDN

In general, you bid per click (and pay per click) on the GDN just as you do on the Search Network. Bids are set at the Ad Group level. If you like, however, you can mix and match targeting methods and raise or lower your bids.

Quality Score on the Display Network suffers from the same contradiction as it does on the Search Network. Google gets paid by the click, and you get paid by the conversion. Accordingly, Google will try to push you to run on lots of sites and write ads that promise "free, free, free" to generate lots of clicks. You want to be very choosy as to which sites you run on, however, and you want to write ads the attract your best customers, and repel tire-kickers and others who are not likely to convert, nor likely to buy high-profit items.

Even before you activate a Display Network campaign, you should exclude various "naughty" websites and apps. The Display Network is full of junk and nefarious websites, so to use it, you must be careful. I recommend that at the account level, therefore, you disable many of the most problematic websites at the very beginning. Once you're running, you also want to check your placements on a regular basis and identify "naughty" websites and apps to exclude them.

Excluding Content Types

Here's how to set universal settings to (hopefully) exclude your ads from being shown next to nefarious and inappropriate content. First, click up to your account level at the "Overview" level. Next, on the left column, click *Settings*. Then in the middle click *Account Settings*. Find *Content exclusions* in the middle and click the down arrow to open the dialogue box. Here's a screenshot:

Content exclusions

Opt out of showing your ads on content that doesn't fit your brand

By default, all video campaigns filter out the most inappropriate or graphic content from all sensitive content categories and content labels. You can customize the filter in the Content exclusions page of campaign settings.

Digital content labels ⑦	Sensitive content ⑦	Content type ⑦
☐ DL-G: General audiences	☐ Tragedy and conflict	☐ Games
☐ Content suitable for families	☐ Sensitive social issues	☐ Live streaming video
☐ DL-PG: Most audiences with parental guidance	☐ Profanity and rough language (Beta for Video campaigns)	☐ Embedded videos
☐ DL-T: Teen and older audiences	☐ Sexually suggestive (Beta for Video campaigns)	☐ Below-the-fold (Display only)
☐ DL-MA: Mature audiences	☐ Sensational and shocking (Beta for Video campaigns)	☐ Parked domains (Display only)
☐ Content not yet labeled		

While content exclusions are completed to the best of our ability, we can't guarantee that all related content will be excluded.

CANCEL   SAVE

Check the most problematic boxes, which are **everything** under "Sensitive content" and under "Content type," the selection for "**Parked domains**." If you do this at the Account level, then Google will attempt to not show your ads on any of these categories across all subordinate Campaigns.

You can also do this at the Campaign level by clicking into a Campaign, and then clicking *Additional settings*. Again, find Content exclusions in the middle and check the boxes for types you don't like. Just remember if you set it at the Campaign level that you have to reset it for each and every Campaign you create. That's why I generally do this at the Account level.

Identify Naughty Placements

On an on-going basis – and at least monthly – you want to identify and exclude "naughty" placements. Some of these appear to be fraudulent websites that live in the Display Network for no purpose other than generating fake clicks, and others are just junk. No one knows for certain, and Google certainly isn't talking. After you've run your Campaign(s) for at least a week, or perhaps a month, you can explore where your ads were placed (called "placements") and block ones that are either inappropriate, have expensive costs per clicks, or poor or expensive conversion rates or any of these problems. Here's how.

Click into a Display Network Campaign that has sufficient data. Click *Placements* on the left column. Click *Where Ads Showed* at the top. You should then see a running table of where your ads are being shown vis-à-vis the time horizon you indicate at the top right (e.g., last month, last thirty days, all time, etc.). *All time* is probably the best choice as a time horizon. Next, click and sort by column; I recommend sorting by Cost first. Here's a screenshot:

Placement	Type	Ad group	Clicks	Impr.	Avg. CPC	↓ Cost
yahoo.com	Site	Hair Transplant	30	46,017	$8.48	$254.51
Mobile App: Word Connect ⌐ (iTunes...	Mobile application	Hair Transplant	17	212	$9.76	$165.91
mercurynews.com	Site	Hair Transplant	7	2,441	$7.22	$50.55
webmd.com	Site	Hair Transplant	5	1,426	$8.29	$41.44

PLACEMENTS   WHERE ADS SHOWED   EXCLUSIONS

All time
Aug 1, 2016 – Jan 3, 2018

Network: YouTube and Display   Filter by

You can also enable columns, including a column for conversions and cost per conversion. Identify websites or apps that are a) costing a lot of money and/or b) have a high cost per click and/or cost per conversion. To block a website or app, just click the checkbox and then *Edit > Exclude* from Campaign. Here's a screenshot:

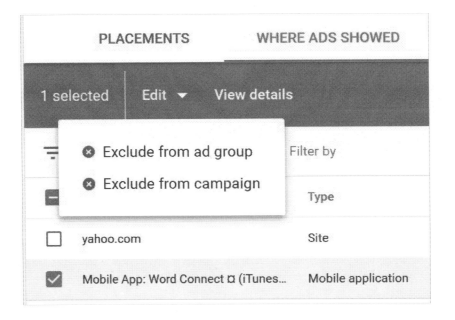

You can also download your placements into Excel, identify the bad / nefarious placements, and then upload a master list into the Shared library. This is located under *Tools > Shared Library > Placement Exclusions* list. Here's a screenshot:

| GO TO | | | ? | | M |

Return to previous AdWords

SHARED LIBRARY

Audience manager

Portfolio bid strategies

Negative keyword lists

Shared budgets

Placement exclusion lists

emarketing   Campaign

If I am working with a client that is heavily using the Display Network, I build up a "Naughty list" of apps and placements in this way and then link the "Naughty list" to all my Display Network campaigns. In this way, you can "inherit" the intelligence from the "Naughty list" from an old campaign to a new one, and avoid the painful and expensive learning curve of finding out the naughty placements.

Once you are running, I recommend checking your Placements at least monthly and then aggregating them into your "Naughty list." This is very important because you will be refining the Display Network to weed out the bad / nefarious websites and over time, you can be much more effective with your Display Network campaigns. As to why Google doesn't do a better job policing its own network, well, I suppose we can wait for a World Communist Revolution against evil corporations or just do it ourselves in the meantime.

>> Monitoring Your GDN Campaigns

The Display Network is full of nefarious sites, bad match types, and just generally a lot of confusion. So if you do decide to run on the GDN, be sure to monitor it closely! If you are running on GDN using keyword targeting, in particular, be sure to monitor your placements and look for nefarious placements – placements that are obviously fraudulent, that generate a lot of clicks, or that generate few conversions (or all three).

Monitor Your Placements

To see your placements, go to *Campaign > Ad Group > Placements > Where Ads Showed.* Here's a screenshot:

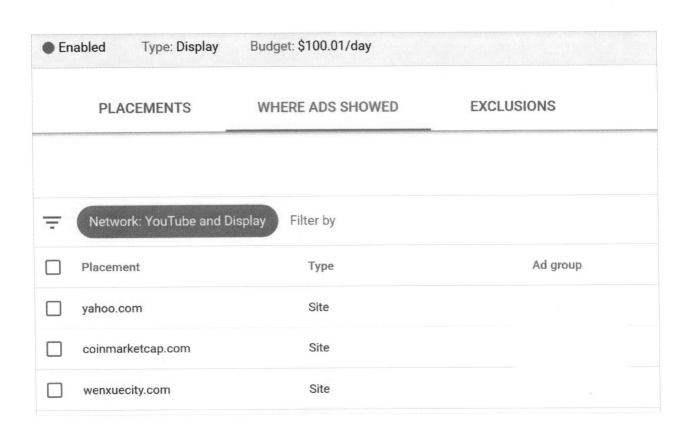

Note that regardless of the targeting method you should periodically check your placements and exclude those that seem irrelevant and/or nefarious.

Enable and Monitor Conversions

In addition, you want to have conversion tracking enabled between AdWords and Google Analytics. In this way, you can see what placements are not just getting clicks but also getting conversions. "Kill your dogs, and let your winners run" is as relevant to the Display Network as to the Search Network. You are constantly looking to identify strong performers (to keep) and weak performers (to terminate). To learn more about conversion tracking in AdWords, see this official Google AdWords video at **http://jmlinks.com/41q**.

Other Metrics

While conversions are the Holy Grail of all advertising on AdWords, you want to be aware that in many cases you won't get immediate conversions. In fact, Display Network campaigns are often run for branding or awareness issues. To that end you want to measure on at least a monthly basis:

Placements by Impressions. Which placements are generating the most impressions? Are they relevant?

Placements by Clicks. Which placements are generating the most clicks? Are they relevant?

Placements by Cost. Which placements are the most expensive? In total, by CPC, and by cost per conversion? Why? Are they worth it?

Placements by Click Thru Rates. Which placements are generating the highest CTRs? Why? Can you increase the impressions on these placements? How?

Placements by Conversions / Conversion Rates. Which placements are generating the highest conversions and conversion rates? Why? Can you increase the impressions on these placements? How?

Consider evaluating your Campaigns by **targeting method** according to the metrics above as well. For example, which targeting method (e.g., Keywords vs. In-market audiences) is generating the highest impressions, clicks, CTR, conversion rate, etc.? As you experiment with your GDN Campaigns look for placements and/or targeting methods that seem to be "working" and expand them, and look for placements and/or targeting methods that do not seem to be "working" and kill them. Another metric that's valuable is the bounce rate on your website. Since a lot of Display Network advertising is about brand-building, look not only at the conversions generated but at the bounce rate and time on site as shown in Google Analytics. If people are clicking through on your GDN ads and checking out your website, then this is indicative of brand-building.

"Let your winners run, and kill your dogs" is as valid on the Display Network as it is on the Search Network. Nurture your winners in terms of targeting methods, placements, and ads. Kill your dogs. Be merciless.

In addition, remember to consider alternatives to the Display Network such as advertising on Facebook, LinkedIn, Twitter, or YouTube and compare results on those "browse" systems against those on the GDN. Identify the best performers and put your money there, and abandon those that do not perform – the GDN may (or may not) be your best venue.

⏩⏩ DELIVERABLE: DISPLAY NETWORK WORKSHEET

The **DELIVERABLE** for this chapter is a completed worksheet on the Google Display Network. You'll investigate whether you want to run on the GDN, at all, and if so, in which ways (especially which targeting method(s) and placements make the most sense).

> For the **worksheet**, go to **https://www.jm-seo.org/workbooks** (click on "AdWords Workbook 2018," enter the code 'adwords18' to register if you have not already done so), and click on the link to the "Google Display Network Worksheet."

6

YouTube

YouTube, owned by Google, is the #1 video site on the Internet and often touted as the #2 search engine, larger than Bing or Yahoo. Everyone – including possibly your customers – uses YouTube – which can make it an incredible advertising opportunity. While you can use text ads and placement targeting on the Display Network to get your text ad on YouTube, you'll do far better if you produce a short video on your product or service and then advertise that video on YouTube. This Chapter focuses on video advertising opportunities on YouTube. (Refer to my *Social Media Marketing Workbook* at **http://jmlinks.com/smm** for a full discussion of *free* opportunities on YouTube).

Let's get started!

TODO LIST:

>> Research Your Customers on YouTube

>> Set up a Channel on YouTube

>> Upload a Video to Your Channel

>> Enable Clickable Links in Your Video

>> Set Up a YouTube Campaign in AdWords

>> Target Your Ad: Video Targeting

>> Evaluate Your YouTube Advertising Performance

>> >> Deliverable: YouTube Advertising Worksheet

Videos on YouTube "live" on a Channel, so to do well on YouTube, you'll need to set up a Channel. (As we explained in Chapter 5, you can use the Google Display Network > Placement targeting to place ads on YouTube but those ads are generally "crowded out" by video ads on YouTube). To get started to see if YouTube could be good for you, do some **research** to decide if your target customers are "on" YouTube, and, if so, what they are doing. Everyone is "on YouTube" sooner or later, but in general, you'll get the best advertising performance if one or the following criteria apply:

- **Search**. People are likely to search YouTube pro-actively. "How to" searches such as "How to get a puppy to stop biting" or "How to truss a turkey" are very popular on YouTube, so if your company produces something that explains "how to do something," or if your market is adjacent to "how to" searches, then YouTube can be good. An example would be a cooking gadget company that could advertise on "how to" cooking videos, a dog training company that can advertise on "how to" training videos for dogs, or a physical fitness supplement company that can advertise on "how to" videos for crunches or pushups

ARE YOUR CUSTOMERS ON YOUTUBE?

- **Browse**. People are going onto YouTube to watch videos on thousands of topics, and you can demographically target them. For example, let's say you marketed Donald Trump paraphernalia, you'd know that many Trump supporters and political junkies go on YouTube to keep up with politics, and watch certain kinds of videos or certain kinds of channels. (The same would go for political junkies of the Left). Or, suppose you're targeting young adults, and you know that they are big consumers of music videos. It can also be very specific such as targeting fishermen / women who watch YouTube for fishing videos (as there are TONS of fishing / outdoors videos on YouTube).

Before you decide to set up a Channel or advertise, you want to **research** whether your target customers are on YouTube, and if so, whether they are *searching* and/or *browsing* video content.

- If they're searching, what types of keywords searches are they doing?

- If they're browsing, what type of videos are they watching?

Keyword Research

Unfortunately, there isn't a YouTube-only keyword discovery tool (like the Google AdWords Keyword Planner) that focuses only on search volumes on YouTube. You have to use the generic AdWords Keyword Planner.

So return to AdWords, and go to *Tools > Keyword Planner*. Generally, if a search has a "how to" flavor to it and it's visual, you can bet it will be searched on YouTube. Secondly, go to YouTube, and just start typing. Pay attention to YouTube's autocomplete. Anything that ranks high there is a good bet as well to have some search volume on YouTube. Here's a screenshot for "bass fishing" autocomplete on YouTube:

bass fishing

bass fishing **tips and techniques**
bass fishing **with frogs**
bass fishing **tournament**
bass fishing **videos**
bass fishing **tips**
bass fishing **in the winter**
bass fishing **with plastic worms**
bass fishing **challenge**
bass fishing **in ponds**
bass fishing **2017**

Revisit your Keyword Worksheet and add a tab for YouTube. Brainstorm core keywords and ad groups that reflect how people search YouTube. As you browse videos that pop up on YouTube for searches relevant to your product or service, pay attention to the

view count of videos. For example, if you search on YouTube for *bass fishing*, you'll see this video at or near the top:

You'll notice that it has 440,000 views, which means a lot of people are searching for and watching videos on bass fishing. If you see many videos relevant to your product or service with (relatively) high view counts, you know that YouTube may be a great marketing tool for you. If not, not.

Finding Video Volume for Browsing

You may decide that **search** isn't that important on YouTube, but you do suspect that people are **browsing** and watching videos on YouTube. You can search YouTube directly to look at video volume and engagement. To do this, go to YouTube, and then enter in a search keyword such as "fishing." Next, click on *Filters* at the top right, and select *Sort By > View Count*. You can also click back to Filters, and select *This Year* to look at the highest videos for the last twelve months.

BROWSE AND VIEW VIDEOS TO DETERMINE VIDEO VOLUME

Another way is to scroll down on the left column, to *Browse Channels*. Here, you'll see broad categories of videos such as *Beauty & Fashion* or *Sports*. You can click into individual channels to browse popular videos and get a sense of the channel subscribers. These are much broader categories than searching by keywords, but they can give you a sense of whether or not your target customers are active on YouTube. You can also click on *Trending* on the top left to see what's trending.

However, as you browse YouTube, don't fall into the trap of assuming that you have to be in a "mega" industry like pop music to make it work for you. Many people watch videos in very nichey ways in YouTube such as quilters who want to learn how to quilt, teenagers who want to put on eye makeup, and fishermen (and women) who want to learn how to be better anglers, so "riches are in the niches" on YouTube just as on Google.

Your research process is:

> Are my customers watching YouTube videos in a targeted way?
>
> If so, what is the target? What keywords, channels, and video topics?

Make a list of channels, videos, and keywords that identify "where your customers" hang out on YouTube. This will become your targeting strategy.

▶ SET UP A CHANNEL ON YOUTUBE

Assuming you've decided that, yes, your customers are on YouTube and, yes, you'd like to give YouTube advertising a go, the next best step is to set up a Channel. The easiest way to do this is to sign up for a Google Account via Gmail. I'd recommend that you use the **same** email that you use to login to AdWords, if at all possible. (You can and should link your YouTube and AdWords account (see **http://jmlinks.com/41k)**). Using the same email address for both is the easiest and best, however. Alternatively, you can also create a brand new YouTube account.

Here are your steps:

1. Go to **https://www.gmail.com/** and sign up for a Gmail account, if you don't have a Gmail you already use for corporate stuff on Google.
2. Alternatively, you can set up a Google account and link this to any email such as **yourname@company.com**. To do this, read the help file at **http://jmlinks.com/25j**.
3. Next, visit **http://jmlinks.com/25k** and follow the instructions to "Create a channel with a business or other name."

Populate your Channel with a nice-looking cover photo, icon, and fill out the contact information on the "About" tab. You now have a YouTube channel!

▶▶ UPLOAD A VIDEO TO YOUR CHANNEL

Although you can advertise on Google with just text ads (via the Google Display Network > Managed Placements or read the AdWords help file at **http://jmlinks.com/27e**), you'll do much better if you create a short video that promotes your company or product. The best ads are short and to the point, quickly explaining who you are, what you have to offer, and why a person on YouTube should care.

The sky's the limit on video production. You can Google "videographers" in your local area to find people to help you shoot a short video. You can use tools such as Camtasia, iMovie, and Windows Movie Maker. You can use services such as Fiverr to find video editors, and you can literally just Google "make a video ad for YouTube" and read the ads and organic results.

YouTube even has a simple app, called the 'YouTube Director for business app' that will help you shoot video ads right from your phone. Learn more at **http://jmlinks.com/25m**. YouTube also has a very good mega resource on how to advertise on YouTube at **http://jmlinks.com/41f**. Of course, like all official Google information, it's pretty salesy!

Once you've created your video ad, login to your YouTube channel, and in the top right click on the upwards arrow to upload the video. Be ready with:

- A short video title.
- A short video description, including an *http://* link to your website for more information.
- Keywords to "tag" your video.

Create a "Custom Thumbnail" by clicking "Custom Thumbnail" (this may not show on a brand new Channel). I recommend a simple, easy-to-read Video Thumbnail as this will show up as your ad on YouTube search and as a recommended video. Here's a screenshot of how a video ad looks on YouTube search:

You can read the official YouTube help on how to create custom thumbnails at **http://jmlinks.com/27f**.

Once the video is uploaded and approved by YouTube, find your video, you'll need to copy / paste the URL at the top of the page. It should look something like **https://www.youtube.com/watch?v=CRB6w4Dmjdw**.

What Makes a Good YouTube Ad?

What makes a good video ad on YouTube? First and foremost, of course, it's in **video** format. So it's short and **visual** and very quickly and very clearly explains your business proposition. A wise YouTuber once told me to think "street performance art" and not "movie" when making a good video for YouTube. What did he mean?

1. **Make the video short.** People are "in a hurry" to something else, and they aren't signing up for a long movie format. Short is better than long. I'd recommend one minute or less.
2. **Make it simple.** Use 6th grade English, not Ph.D. level English. Be very succinct and to the point. Don't beat around the bush.
3. **Make it (visually) provocative**. You have to get them to STOP and take a look. They're not signing up for the latest Meryl Streep movie in which they pay their money, get their popcorn, and are willing to sit through twenty minutes of previews and some long and pompous introduction before getting to the action. You have to get them to STOP by nearly shouting: HEY LOOK AT ME! THIS IS WEIRD, CRAZY, INCREDIBLE (without destroying your brand image).
4. **Have a defined next step or action**. What do you want them to do after they watch your video? A probate attorney, for example, wants to explain a little about probate and then get them to click FROM the video TO her website, where she wants them to register for a FREE CONSULT. So she'd literally say something in the video like, "Probate is crazy complicated, so click the link in the video description to request a FREE CONSULT with my office!"

And of course, a good video is **good-looking**. But here you don't' really need a slick, professionally produced video as much as a video that is **authentic**. People want to know that you really "know your stuff" about probate law, for example, and that trust that you create gets them to take the next action. They really don't care about your hairstyle or the lighting, though, <u>good sound is a must</u>.

Go search and browse YouTube and watch some ads that are close to what you and your company would like to promote. Pay attention to how the ads a) grab your attention quickly, b) communicate their value proposition, and c) lead to a "next step" or "desired action." A good resource is AdWeek's list of the most popular ads on YouTube, as for example at **http://jmlinks.com/41h**. Another good resource is "Why Storyboard?" from YouTube at **http://jmlinks.com/41j**.

Once you have your video ad produced, you can upload your video to your Channel. Give your video a short, to-the-point headline and write a short, to-the-point description. Be sure to have a good-looking and catchy thumbnail image.

» ENABLE CLICKABLE LINKS IN YOUR VIDEO

Be sure to include a clickable link in your video description, preferably right after the first sentence, and in the format of **http://www.yourwebsite.com/**. It MUST be in the *http://* format to be clickable! You can then reference the link for "more information" in your short video ad, such as telling the viewer, "Click on the link in the video description to learn more!"

Here's a screenshot from one of my videos (at **http://jmlinks.com/27g**) showing a clickable URL in the video description, using the **http://tinyurl.com** shortener:

Published on Sep 16, 2016
Master SEO for your business in this up-to-date tutorial on Search Engine Optimization basics. (For free materials, including the SEO TOOLBOOK go to http://tinyurl.com/j666q9j). Search Engine Optimization is explained in this easy tutorial or SEO guide, starting with how to define the best keywords, going thru page tags, and even discussing how to never stop learning. Learn the 2017 tips, tricks, and tools in this easy tutorial or guide.

In addition, you can add "cards" to your video. "Cards" on YouTube are clickable links in the video itself. To add a "card" to your video:

- Click on your logo on the top right of YouTube, when you are logged into your Channel.
- Click on Creator Studio, and then click on Video Manager on the left-hand menu.
- Find your video and click edit.

YouTube "Cards" are
Clickable Links in a Video

Click on "Cards" to enable YouTube's "Cards" feature, and insert text, an image, and a link to your website URL.

> **VIDEO.** Watch a video on how to use annotations, cards, and overlays into a YouTube video at **http://jmlinks.com/25n**. You can read the official Google help file on YouTube cards at **http://jmlinks.com/27h**.

Cards appear in the top right of a YouTube video and "pop out" when they appear. Users can click on them to learn more and then click from the card to your website. Here's a screenshot showing the card in the top right corner:

(Note: YouTube has discontinued *annotations* and *call-to-action overlays*, so it is best to add only *cards* going forward). At this point, you've created a Channel, uploaded a video advertising your company or product, and inserted *http://* links in the video description, and at least one card for more information.

You're ready to return to AdWords!

▶▶ SET UP A YOUTUBE CAMPAIGN IN ADWORDS

If you already have a *Campaign > Ad Group* on YouTube, you can skip this section. If not, to create a video campaign, login to AdWords, and click the blue circle. Select *Video* as the campaign type. Select one of the three options – *Product and brand consideration, Brand awareness and reach,* or *Without a goal.* The first two give you step-by-step instructions, while the third option is totally do-it-yourself. Follow the steps to define:

Campaign Name. Give it an easy-to-remember name such as *Cat Boarding: YouTube.* I recommend you put YouTube at the end so you can see at an instant that this is a YouTube Campaign and not a Search or Display Campaign.

Budget. Set up a daily budget. Just as on regular AdWords, you specify a maximum spend per day.

Networks. Here, you need to make an important choice –

> **YouTube search results**. Use this option to show your video when someone pro-actively searches on YouTube. (*Must be used in combination with the next option*).

> **YouTube videos**. Use this option more when people are in "browse" mode to show your video before, after, or along videos as people browse. (*Must be used in combination with the first option*).

> **Video Partners in the Display Network**. I do not recommend this option, so uncheck it. Here you have the same problem with click fraud and nefarious sites as on the Google Display Network.

Ad Group. Create an Ad Group, again reflecting your product or service (keyword) organization such as *Cat Boarding, Cat Grooming,* or *Cat Toys* and name it appropriately as for example *Cat Boarding: YouTube – Keywords,* or *Cat Boarding: YouTube – Remarketing.*

Bidding. Set a bid per view. Note that on YouTube you pay by the *video view*, not by the click. YouTube uses what they call "TrueView" pricing meaning you pay if, and only if, the user watches your video for at least thirty seconds or to the end of the video, or if it's a search ad if they click on the video and/or an action. See **http://jmlinks.com/41g** for a full explanation.

Targeting. Leave these options blank for now, as we will discuss in detail. These are marked as *People who you want to reach* and *Content where you want your ads to show.*

Create your video ad. Enter the exact URL of the video you want to promote here. Select a format such as *In-stream ad* or *bumper ad* ("browse mode") or *video discovery* ("search mode") ad. Write a headline and description. Select a landing page; I recommend that you use *Your YouTube channel page.*

Again, similarly to regular AdWords, Google stupidly makes you go through every step even if you are not ready. Once a *Campaign > Ad Group* is created, however, you can then insert new Ad Groups and Ads much more easily, adjust targeting, etc. Just go through the steps to create your first *Campaign > Ad Group > Ad* and then it will be much easier to manage. What's stupid about this is you only have to do this the very first time, and then from then on it's much easier to manage.

At the end of this process you should have your first *Campaign > Ad Group > Ad*. Pause it so that it doesn't start running until you are completely ready.

Location Targeting in YouTube

You can geotarget on YouTube! For example, Jason's Cat Boarding Emporium could target people watching "cat videos" who also live in San Francisco. Or a pet store could target people watching videos on dog and puppy training who live in Oakland, Berkeley, or El Cerrito, California.

LOCATION TARGETING WORKS IN YOUTUBE

Geotargeting makes it easy to get your ads right to people near your local business and is one of the most exciting features in YouTube advertising. Accordingly, select your

Geotarget (e.g., United States, or drill down to a specific city or state). You do this by being at the Campaign level and selecting *Locations* on the left. For example, since I am only interested in people who live in San Francisco and have cats, I could target cat videos on YouTube but by setting the geotarget to San Francisco, only people who are physically in San Francisco would see my ads. This is a fantastic feature to YouTube advertising as you can have your cake and eat it too – meaning target very broad video types (e.g., "cat videos") but to very narrow locations (e.g., "San Francisco").

Mobile Bid Adjustment

You can also control your mobile bid adjustment in YouTube, if you do / do not want to run on phones and/or tablets. Once you've created a Campaign, click on *Devices* on the left and configure your device targeting by setting bid adjustments up or down. An example here might be a probate attorney who would figure that the most serious people would be watching her videos on their computers, and so she would set a bid adjustment of negative 100% for mobile. If you think there is a strong pattern between mobile vs. desktop vs. tablet, this is yet another useful YouTube targeting refinement.

▶▶ TARGET YOUR AD: VIDEO TARGETING

Now that you've inputted your ad to YouTube, it's time to dive into targeting options. Targeting "lives" at the Ad Group level, just as in regular AdWords. Click into your Ad Group on YouTube, and you'll see targeting options on the left. As with the Display Network, it's a best practice not to mix and match targeting options (though you can in some situations). Let's review targeting options.

> **Keywords.** Here, similar to the Display Network, enter **keywords** that you think someone might be searching on YouTube and/or that might describe similar or adjacent videos. **This is the most common and most powerful way to target your videos.** So in our *Cat Boarding* example, we'd enter keywords like *cats, cat boarding, cat care, kittens*, etc. Google has taken away a lot of YouTube targeting features, so I wouldn't worry about plus signs, quote marks, etc., just enter keywords and remember that, as on the Display Network, the targeting is pretty loose on YouTube.
>
> **Audiences.** Here You can choose people based on:
>
>> **Affinity.** Just as on the Display Network, these are people Google identifies based on their long-term interests. Click to drill into this, and

you'll see groupings like Banking & Finance, Beauty & Wellness, and you can even drill into subgroups.

Intent and life events. The most interesting one here is *In-marketing audiences* which stands for people who are "in the market" for something like an automobile or baby products. Life events refers to milestones like college graduation or marriage.

Remarketing. This leverages your remarketing audience. So, for example, you can "tag" people who visit your website and then show them your video ad as they browse YouTube videos.

Demographics. Here you can target (or exclude) by age group. So you can target, for example, people who are 55-64 with ads on probate or retirement issues.

Topics This is very similar to audiences and attempts to target people based on things that interest them like games, health, fitness, etc.

Placements. This is unique on YouTube. You can find videos or channels that allow advertising and then copy / paste their URLs here. However, if a channel or video is not "monetized" (meaning that the owner does not allow YouTube to place ads), this is all in vain. So double-check to see if you see ads on any relevant placements. Google doesn't enable clickable links here, so open up a new browser window and search YouTube by Channel or Video name to find out if it allows advertising. If you see ads, it does. If you don't, it doesn't.

» EVALUATE YOUR YOUTUBE ADVERTISING PERFORMANCE

Once your ads are up and running on YouTube, evaluating the performance is similar to the rest of the Display Network. Click into an Ad Group. Then, along the left column, click:

Keywords to browse the keywords the triggered your video ads. As elsewhere on AdWords, you can create "negative keywords" to block your ad.

Audiences to learn characteristics about the audiences reached.

Demographics to see age information (if available).

Topics to see topics.

Placements and then *Where ads showed* to see which videos / channels ran your ad. As on the Display Network, you can block your ad from placements.

You can also go into Google Analytics to view clicks coming from YouTube to evaluate what happens "after the click." To do this, create a Segment by clicking on the *Segments* tab in Google Analytics, and then *Custom*, and source as *YouTube.com*.

And within your YouTube Channel, you can click into *Creator Studio > Analytics* to browse information about your videos.

VIDEO. Watch a video on how to set up Segments in Google Analytics at **http://jmlinks.com/25p**.

Returning back to your YouTube Channel (not AdWords, and not Google Analytics), you can go to *Creator Studio > Analytics* and then drill down into an individual video to see key performance indicators such as watch time, view duration, views, geographies, genders, traffic sources, and playback locations. In summary, there is really a wealth of information in AdWords, Analytics, and YouTube about what happens with your videos!

►►► DELIVERABLE: YOUTUBE ADVERTISING WORKSHEET

The **DELIVERABLE** for this chapter is a completed worksheet on YouTube advertising. You'll investigate whether you want to run on YouTube, at all, and if so, in which ways (especially which targeting method(s) and placements make the most sense).

For the **worksheet**, go to **https://www.jm-seo.org/workbooks** (click on "AdWords Workbook 2018," enter the code 'adwords18' to register if you have not already done so), and click on the link to the "YouTube Advertising Worksheet."

THIS PAGE INTENTIONALLY LEFT BLANK

(PONDER IT)

7

METRICS

Making money on AdWords is easy! *Just make $1.01 for every $1.00 you spend, and you'll make money each and every day!* It's not quite that simple, of course, as the line between "what you're spending on AdWords" and "what you're getting in sales" can be pretty fuzzy. Even worse, Google AdWords "support" is always there – *like a good bartender* – egging you on to keep spending on *clicks* and *branding*, when really you should focus on *conversions* (defined as either *sales* on an e-Commerce website or completed *sales inquiry* forms for more complicated products or services). In this Chapter, we'll dive into how to measure your performance on AdWords, and how to use AdWords metrics to improve your return on investment (ROI) continually and/or your *return on ad spend* or **ROAS**. Be forewarned: *you may know what you want to know but not actually be able ever to know it*, so to speak. Or *not know it fully*; so you'll need to combine some hard metrics with some soft gut instinct. "Half of my advertising dollars are wasted," so the saying goes; "I just don't know which half."

Let's get started!

TODO LIST:

» ROI: Make $1.01 for Every $1.00 You Spend

» ROI: It Gets Complicated

» Spot Check Your Ads

» Check Your Spending Metrics

» Monitor the Display Network and/or YouTube

» Set up Goals in Google Analytics

» Set up Conversion Tracking in AdWords or Google Analytics

>> Review Your Conversion Data in AdWords

>> Identify Problems and Opportunities

>>>> Deliverable: An AdWords Metrics Worksheet

>> ROI: MAKE $1.01 FOR EVERY $1.00 YOU SPEND

Conceptually and in a perfect world, your **Return on Investment (ROI)** from AdWords is deceptively simple:

For every $1.00 in ad spend, make at least $1.01 in profit.

But in reality, this equation is very complicated. On the **spend** side, you can certainly see how much you are paying for impressions and for clicks, and you can correlate both impressions and clicks to keyword search queries (*on the Search Network*) and placements (*on the Google Display Network*). You can very easily see what you're spending on a daily, weekly, or monthly basis for clicks and impressions and correlate that with keywords or placements. These are what I call your **Spending Metrics**. (Note: in a perfect world, you'd also calculate and include the cost of you and your employees' labor spent setting up and managing your AdWords account, but we'll ignore those costs).

Conversion Metrics

Your profit from AdWords, however, depends not on your *Spending Metrics* but on your **Conversion Metrics**. Here we have to move from the *what's-easy-to-measure* (your spend) to *what's-hard-to-measure* (your sales).

Let's take a simple scenario of a customer who comes back from vacation in Mexico, had a great time, picks up his cat at Jason's Cat Emporium, and wants to reward his Kitty with a brand new cat collar. He goes to Google, searches for *cat collars*, finds our e-Commerce store and makes a purchase.

We have:

Google search query: *Cat Collars*

He sees our ad for "Amazing Cat Collars" and clicks. (Behind the scenes, we have pre-identified the search query "cat collars" and bid $2.00 for the click. We "win" the auction and pay Google $1.75 for that click, one penny more than the next highest bid for the click on Google).

He purchases the cat collar for $10.00. (Our cost is $4.00, which we pay to our Mexican cat collar partner (*as the collars are made in Mexico, where he could have bought the cat collar for just $1.00 – but that's another story; we'll also ignore shipping and other costs for this simple example*)). Our profit per collar is thus $6.00.

So, on the vendor side, we have this equation to calculate our ROI:

Revenue from the sale of the collar from the customer: **$10.00**.

Cost of collar (paid to our Mexican supplier) **$4.00**

Cost of click (paid to Google): **$1.75**

Profit = ($10.00 -$4.00) - $1.75 = $4.25.

ROI is calculated as ($10.00 - $4.00) - $1.75 / $1.75 = 2.42 = 242%

(meaning you more than DOUBLED your money).

ROI as a formula is *Profit -Advertising Cost / Advertising Cost* expressed as a percentage. You want a positive, big number!

Now, this formula assumes that, first, you can actually determine the data inputs (costs, in particular, can be hard to determine), and, second, that this is a sale you got from AdWords and AdWords alone (meaning, you wouldn't have gotten it if you didn't advertise). Those are assumptions that are not always easy to meet or determine in the real world.

That said, a focus on ROI tells you to keep your eye on making at least $1.01 for every $1.00 in incremental spend on AdWords. It's a good but unrealistic goal. And, don't forget, the *lifetime value of a customer*. Even if you "lose" money on an AdWords ad, if the lifetime value of that customer is substantial, it may be OK to "lose" money on that first click (which gets you a customer) because subsequently that customer will come back to your website (and your business) without having to click through on any ads.

Calculating Your Maximum Bid

How much can we pay Google for a click on AdWords and still make money?

Assuming a 100% conversion rate (that is, that EVERY click to our website leads to a purchase), then we can safely bid up to $5.99 and make a profit. For example, if the click cost $5.99 and the collar costs us $4.00, then we would make $.01 from each sale of the $10.00 Kitty collar.

Our **ROI** is *Profit -Advertising Cost / Advertising Cost* expressed as a percentage or $6.00 (our profit per collar) - $5.99 (cost of the click)/ $5.99 (cost of the click) = .16% (return on our money). We're positive, or (barely) in the black.

Once we spend MORE than $6.00 on the click, our ROAS goes negative. If, for example, we spend $7.00 on the click, then our ROAS is $6.00 - $7.00 / $7.00 = -14%. We're negative, or in the red.

Not All Clicks Convert

But here's where it gets complicated, even with a simple e-Commerce website. First and foremost, not every click ends in a sale!

If our conversion rate is 50%, then we can only pay half as much for a click ($5.99 / 2 = $2.95) because half our clicks fail to end up in sales, and so on and so forth. The lower our conversion rate, the less we can bid per click. And, of course, the lower our profit, the less we can bid for clicks, too. (*If our Mexican supplier raises the price of the collar to $7.00 from $4.00 then, accordingly, we have to pay less per click to break even.*)

The *Cost Per Click* must be less than the *Profit Per Click* for you to make money on AdWords, or turning that around your *Profit Per Click* must be greater than your *Cost Per Click*:

Cost Per Click < Profit Per Click

Or

Profit Per Click > Cost Per Click

And the Profit Per Click is the *profit per sale times the conversion rate.*

Profit Per Click = Profit Per Sale X Conversion Rate

If, for example, we make $6.00 per sale of a collar, and we have a 100% conversion rate, then our profit per click is $6.00. But if we have a 50% conversion rate, then our profit per click is cut in half, becoming $6.00 x .50 = $3.00. With a 100% conversion rate, we can bid up to $5.99 to "get the click," but with a 50% conversion rate we can only bid $2.99 per click, and so on. In most cases, your conversion rate will be much, much lower than 50%, more like 2% or 3%, so with a 2% conversion rate, our profit per click is

$6.00 (the profit of each collar) x .02 (the conversion rate) = .12 or 12¢ per click!

Turning this around, if we "bought" 100 clicks on Google that would cost us 100 x .12 = $12.00, and with a 2% conversion rate those 100 clicks would have generated two sales at $6.00 each, so we would break even at any CPC < .02.

If you want to dive more deeply into these equations, I recommend that you check out Google's Chief Economist, Hal Varian, and his video that explains how your bidding strategy should intersect with your profits.

VIDEO. Watch a video on ROI on Google AdWords by Google's Chief Economist, Hal Varian at **http://jmlinks.com/25q**.

Mr. Varian goes way into the details on ROI and bidding strategy, but let's keep it simple and summarize what you, as an advertiser, can actually attempt to measure and then attempt to improve on in the real world:

Measure:

- Your **AdWords costs** measured as cost per click vis-à-vis specific keywords, landing pages, and products or services.
- The **revenue** and **profit** (*revenue minus expenses*) of the related product or service; or, if you're measuring a sales lead, the imputed value of that sales lead to your ultimate product or service.

Improve on AdWords:

- **Decrease** your cost per click through **better bidding**.
- Identify **keywords that convert** ("winners") vs. keywords that do not convert ("dogs"), and *let your winners run, and shoot your dogs*. Ditto for ads; identify high performing vs. low performing ads.
  - Pay attention not only to the **conversion rate** (i.e., *which clicks end in sales or sales leads*) but also which products or services generate **more profit** vis-à-vis your AdWords spend, that is higher *quality* keyword patterns.
- **Write Better Ads.** Write better ads that "attract" high-value, converting customers and "repel" low-value, non-converting customers as well as ads that have a sufficiently high CTR (Click Thru Rate) to get you a better Quality Score.
- **Improve your landing page experience** and **conversion rate** so that you not only get clicks to your landing page, but a higher percentage of those clicks convert to a sale and/or sales lead.

This last point is important. You won't always get an immediate sale or sales lead, so brainstorm not only what sale / sales lead you want but also **intermediate steps** that can help you "capture" the name / email / phone of a prospect so that your sales staff can work on turning a mere *prospect* into a paying *customer*. Free downloads, free eBooks, free software, and even "sign up for our incredibly interesting email newsletter" can also be considered conversions.

ONCE YOU'VE GOT THE CLICK, GET SOMETHING FOR IT

In terms of strategy vis-à-vis metrics:

> Once you've received the click from Google, do everything possible to capture your customers' contact information, start a relationship or conversation with them, etc.

You want to use AdWords to **build your email / phone prospect list**, even if it's not an immediate sale! Throughout, don't focus so much on clicks, and the click thru rate as much as on cost-per-click, conversion rate, and the value of each conversion.

» ROI: It Gets Complicated

Just make more money per click than you're spending per click! That's in the hypothetical *Hal-Varian-Google-economist make-believe world* that Google lives in. But you and I live in the real world, and we often do not have the required data at our fingertips. If we're running an e-Commerce store, we may have a good idea of the profit per sale, and we can get the conversion rate from Google Analytics or our e-Commerce platform. We're in the strongest position to really know how much we can pay per click.

Some Clicks Convert (Just Not Immediately)

However, even at the best e-Commerce store, not every click will immediately end in a sale; some visitors may leave the website, and come back days or even weeks later, and then purchase. So what looks like a failure (no conversion) may actually be a conversion. Google Analytics and AdWords do attempt to track customers for 30 days giving you some conversion data in a 30-day window, but it is far from perfect.

Lifetime Customer Value (LCV) and Gut Instinct

In addition, a customer may "find you" one time through Google AdWords and then become a "customer for life." So the lifetime customer value (LCV) may be far, far more than the simple value from that immediate click to sale conversion on AdWords. You need to pay attention to this metric, and you can't expect an immediate click to sale behavior, especially for complicated or expensive products like Disney Cruises or Toyota Camrys. On the negative side, it may be that the customer already found you via SEO / organic reach on Google or perhaps word of mouth (first), and then clicked on your ad.

In this case, Google is falsely attributing to AdWords a sale that you "would have gotten anyway" from this customer.

> Some factors (e.g., some clicks convert not at first but after a period of back-and-forth) indicate that your *revenue from AdWords is higher* than actually reported in the data.

> And some factors (e.g., AdWords falsely takes credit for sales you would have gotten anyway through SEO or word of mouth) indicate that your *revenue from AdWords is lower* than actually reported in the data.

My feeling, therefore, is to *take the data seriously* but to *take it also with a grain of salt* (yes, I know that's a contradiction!). Your "gut instinct" as to whether AdWords is working is as important as any "hard" data that your data wonks and Hal Varian can come up with.

ROAS: Return on Ad Spend

Another metric that people like to use is called *ROAS* or *Return on Ad Spend*. This is a simpler, "back of the napkin," way to measure your AdWords performance. The formula to calculate ROAS is:

ROAS = revenue from ad campaign / cost of ad campaign

So if your ad campaign generates $10,000 in revenue and costs your $1,000 you have:

ROAS = $10,000/$1,000 = 10 or 1000%.

For a quick, online ROAS calculator visit **http://jmlinks.com/41m**. The problem with ROAS, however, is that it ignores cost. You can generate revenue with AdWords yet still lose money if you don't calculate the costs that go into getting those clicks (i.e., AdWords costs) as well as your own costs of production. So, while the industry often focuses on ROAS, I recommend you focus on ROI instead (at least conceptually).

And, throughout, realize that you often can do no better than "back of the napkin" calculations as to whether you are making money, or not, with your AdWords investment. Those that run very tight and easy e-commerce stores are in the best position to calculate their ROI, but most of us (even in e-commerce) will have some "variables" that we do not know for certain. Do your best.

Beyond e-Commerce: Feedback Forms and Sales Leads

Many of us will not be running e-Commerce sites, however. We will measure the performance of our websites in terms of completed feedback forms or sales inquiries. A law firm, for example, will want to use Google AdWords to generate clicks for the search query "Personal Injury Lawyer Tulsa" and measure the performance by incoming sales leads off of a web form. Ditto for a Kansas City plumber, who would want his ads on Google to generate inbound web forms or telephone calls.

How much is a completed web form worth? Well, in an ideal world, you'd know the value of the potential lawsuit (or potential plumbing project) plus the probability that your firm is going to win, and you'd deflate all that by your conversion rate (as the client could potentially take his or her lawsuit or plumbing project somewhere else). There's little to no probability in the "real world" that you'll be able to do anything much better than guestimate these numbers. So, sorry, Hal Varian, the equations don't work because we don't have the necessary data, and we never will!

You may never have all the required data. So get over it, and use gut instinct

The best you can do is decide how much you're willing to pay for a completed feedback form via AdWords and calculate your conversion rate based on the clicks that come from AdWords to your website.

Sales Leads Are Valuable: Do Not Undervalue Them!

For businesses that depend on feedback forms, I'd recommend setting a ballpark figure as to the value of each completed feedback form and judging AdWords vs. this figure. However, in my experience, most companies VASTLY devalue the cost that they should pay for a lead.

Don't Underestimate the Value of a "Sales Lead"

Companies will say (with no data to back them up), "we're willing to pay $10.00 for a feedback form," when the value of that "lead" can be $1,000 or $10,000, so please try to get your team to be reasonable about the true value of a completed feedback form. In fact, I'd recommend multiplying that value by 2x or even 12x as, in my experience, most companies vastly underestimate the true value of leads!

Compare AdWords, for example, with other forms of advertising like participation at industry trade shows. To go to a trade show you have the cost of the booth space, the cost of the booth set up, employees' time and travel, etc., and you might get just a few hundred (if that) inquiries from your trade show expense. Each "lead" at the trade show might be costing you literally hundreds or thousands of dollars, compared with a "lead" form AdWords that might just cost you $25.00 or $75.00 or something like that. So, be fair to AdWords, and recognize just how expensive (and how valuable) sales inquiries can be to your business across different advertising and marketing venues.

Visits, Bounces, and Telephone Calls

Another big problem is **call tracking**. In many industries such as plumbers, lawyers, and roofing companies, the person is most likely to do a Google search, land on your website, check your reviews, and then call you on the phone. That phone call "originated" from AdWords, but it isn't easy to track. Google has call-tracking inside of AdWords (if you enable call extensions or click to call on mobile), but realistically, very few people will call right off of an ad. They want first to visit your website. Companies like CallRail (**http://www.callrail.com**) and CallTrackingMetrics (**http://www.calltrackingmetrics.com**), can enable call tracking on your website and feed that data into AdWords. Even so, you have the problem that many people will do a Google search, click, visit your site, leave, come back days or weeks later, and then engage. So the visits, bounces, and call tracking problems can make it "seem" like you have fewer conversions from AdWords than you really have had.

Time on Site, Branding, and Other Metrics

After e-Commerce sales and completed feedback forms, other valuable goals for your website can be signups to your email lists, engagements on social media (e.g., "liking" your company Facebook page), or even time on site. Some companies, especially big ones, look at advertising as a branding experience and aren't that interested in clicks. You might measure impressions (especially on the Google Display Network) as a KPI (Key Performance Indicator) of brand awareness. Just be careful as only the very biggest companies can afford to throw their money away on "brand awareness" advertising; most medium to small businesses need to show some ROI more significant than impressions.

AdWords is expensive, so I would be very skeptical of these "soft" metrics, with the possible exception of **email sign-ups**.

In summary, be aware that, conceptually, you want a positive ROAS / ROI but, in the real world, you will probably have to follow your gut instinct in combination with some very loosey-goosey data from both AdWords and Google Analytics.

≫ SPOT CHECK YOUR ADS

One of the easiest yet most important metrics to measure is whether your ads are running at all, and how frequently. I recommend you "spot check" your ads manually (especially at first) and then at least twice a month. Sometimes Google will say they're running (*and they're not*) or will say that they're not running (*and they are*). Here are two easy ways to verify your ads are running, especially by changing your location if you are using geotargeting. Have your keywords handy, as you want to spot check your ads against your most valuable keywords.

Method #1. Enable an "incognito session" on your browser. Then, use the SERPS.com location tool at **http://jmlinks.com/25r**. Input your keyword, set a location by city or zip code, and hit search. DO NOT CLICK ON YOUR AD as it will cost you. Just check as indicated below. Unfortunately, sometimes Google won't show any ads in an incognito session. In that case, clear your cookies, go to Google and try searching for your ad using the SERPS.com tool; I often use the Microsoft Edge browser for this purpose, as I regularly use Chrome and Microsoft Edge has a wonderful feature to clear cookies with each session. It's ironic to use the Microsoft Edge browser to check whether Google AdWords are running, but it's a good solution!

Method #2. Use the AdWords Ad Preview and Diagnosis Tool. Log in to AdWords, and click on *Tools > Ad Preview and Diagnosis*. On the right-hand side, enter a city, select Desktop or Mobile, and make sure it's Google.com (Google.ca for Canada).

In both methods, you should see your ad displayed most of the time. Note: vary your city location if you are using geotargeting to confirm that your ad is showing in various cities.

Here's a screenshot showing my ad for *Social Media Expert Witness* with the city set to Tulsa, Oklahoma, and device site to Mobile:

Google will highlight your ad in green to make it easy to find. Generally, you want your ads to be showing in the top positions, which are #1, #2, #3, and #4. If your ad is at the bottom, your bid and/or quality score is too low; if your ad is not showing at all, your bid and/or quality score is even worse. Either up your bid or rewrite your ad / keyword / landing page to improve your quality score, until your ad shows consistently.

Note, however, that often times the tool will say your ad is NOT showing when it fact it IS showing. So you must use a combination of manual searches, the SERPS.com tool, and the Google AdWords Preview Tool to spot check – just be aware that none of these tools is 100% reliable.

Search Impression Share or SIS

Inside of AdWords, there is a valuable metric called "SIS" for "Search Impression Share." Your SIS score measured as a percentage shows how frequently your ad was shown vs. how frequently it was eligible to run. For example, let's say that there are 1,000 searches per month for *cat collars* in the USA and you want to run 100% of the time for those searches.

Available Impressions Per Month: **1000**

Your ad appears on **800** of these impressions

Your SIS is **80%**, meaning your ad ran 80% of the time it was eligible to run.

I recommend you aim for an SIS score of 85% or more, meaning your ad was showing at least 85% of the time. If your ad is running less than about 85% of the time, something is wrong — either your bid is too low, you're hitting your budget constraint, or your quality score is too low. If you're hitting the budget constraint, you'll get a notice "Limited by Budget" in AdWords. It's not a good idea to be limited by budget; if our ROAS /ROI is positive, we want to run "full blast," so either reconfigure to tighter keywords (or placements if you're on the GDN) or increase your budget. (You can also get a notice that says "Below first page bid," and again either increase your bid or improve your quality score. Spot check your ads in both cases to verify that they are / are not / running).

AIM FOR AN SIS > 85%

To figure out the universe of available impressions, divide your impressions by your SIS. So, if your AdWords Campaign shows 800 impressions with an SIS of .80 (or 80%), then the total universe of available impressions was 800/.80 = 1000. To blow your mind further, this data is *more accurate* than the data reported in the Google AdWords Keyword Planner!

Enable SIS

The SIS score is available for Campaigns, Ad Groups, and Keywords, but you must "enable" it as a column. To enable SIS, at the Campaign level, go to Campaigns, and then click on Columns, then Modify Columns. Next, find "Competitive Metrics" and select "Search Impr. Share." I usually then save this set of columns by giving it a name like "SIS," so I can re-enable it each time I log in.

You have to go through the same procedure at the Ad Group and Keyword levels to be able to view SIS there.

Here's a screenshot of SIS at the Campaign level:

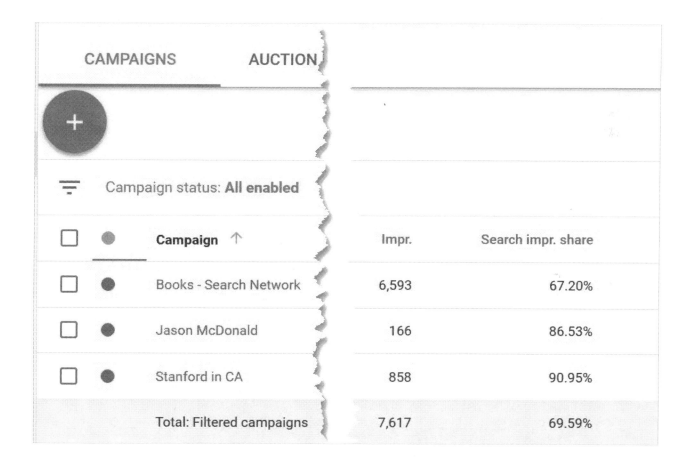

This means that for my "Jason McDonald" campaign (which focuses on high-value expert witness work), I am running at 86.53%. The goal is to run > 85%, which means "full blast." Thus, for my books, you can see I am at 67.20%, meaning they are not running full blast. I thus need to increase my budget or bids, improve my quality score, or otherwise configure this Campaign better. The trick is to do this in such a way that you still generate a positive ROI!

You can check your SIS at every level: Campaign, Ad Group, and Keyword. Thus for a high-value keyword, you can and should check that your SIS is > 85%. If not, you can work on budget, bids, and/or quality score issues.

Position Metric

Next, you want to spot check that your ad position is ideally in the 3-4 range or less, and at worst no greater than four. This means your ad is consistently showing in the top positions as Google shows three to four ads at the top of each page.

This is best seen at the Ad Group level, so drill into the Campaign level so you can look "down" at the Ad Groups that "live" in a Campaign. Find or enable the column called Avg. Pos. for "Average Position." Here's a screenshot of Avg. Position at for Ad Groups that are promoting my books:

Ad group	Clicks	Impr.	CTR	Avg. CPC	Cost	Avg. pos.	Search impr. share
Social Media - Amazon	89	1,350	6.59%	$2.79	$248.60	1.4	89.46%
SEO Workbook - Amazon	79	1,171	6.75%	$1.74	$137.15	1.3	76.33%

This shows that for the Ad Group "Social Media – Amazon," for the last thirty days, I received 89 clicks, 1,350 impressions, had a CTR of 6.59%, and Avg. CPC of $2.79, spent $248.60, was in position 1.4, and had an SIS of 89%. This is really a perfect run across the board. Here's what this means:

1. With an SIS of > 85%, the ads ran all the time.
2. With a position of 1.4, the ads were in the top position.
3. With a CTR of > 1% (at 6.59%) the ads were very engaging to the users.

While conversion tracking is not enabled (because the ads go directly to Amazon), in a perfect world, I'd also measure my raw conversions, my CPA (Cost Per Action, or Conversion), and the revenue or profit generated by those conversions.

Your Goals

Ideally, you want an SIS score of > 85%, and a position of 3-4 as that is the "best value" position in my experience on AdWords. So you increase your bid (or work on your Quality Score) to improve your position and/or your SIS. However, often times, you may need to increase your bid to get your SIS > 85% which will also propel you into the #1 or #2 spots, which means you are overpaying a bit. Or, you bid too low, and then you drop down to #3 or #4 (lower CPC positions), but your SIS goes < 85%, meaning your ad isn't showing.

> The **art** of AdWords is to optimize for an SIS > 85% and a position of 3-4, which is not easy.

If you can't get a position of 3-4, I would prefer an SIS > 85% as you need your ad to show to get results.

▶▶ CHECK YOUR SPENDING METRICS

It goes without saying that you should pay attention to your CPC (Cost Per Click), as you want to minimize your CPC. Check the columns:

Clicks = how many clicks your Campaign / Ad Group / Keyword / Ad received.

Impressions = how many impressions (how much it was seen) vs. SIS. If your SIS is > 85%, then essentially you are showing "all the time." If your SIS is < 85%, then there is more ad inventory, and you can show your ad more.

CTR = click-thru rate. Higher is better. Shoot for at least 1%, but I like to see 3, 4, or even 7% or higher CTRs for tightly focused *Keywords > Ad Groups > Ads*.

Cost = how much you've spent, total, for the time period you've selected in the Top Right.

Cost / conversions / cost per conversion. We'll discuss this in a moment, but this is your conversion data (meaning e-Commerce sales or completed feedback forms).

As you spot check your ads, you're seeking to REDUCE your bid per click YET get your ad to show (SIS > 85%) and maintain your position < 4 and maintain a decent CTR. It's a see-saw and takes weekly or monthly maintenance at first. Once you have a good setup (Campaign > Keyword Focus > Ad Group > Keywords > Ads), then LET YOUR WINNERS RUN but KILL YOUR DOGS. Meaning, once you get an SIS > 85%, an Average Position of < 4, and a CTR of > 1% or more, LEAVE IT ALONE, whether this is a Campaign, an Ad Group, a Keyword, or an Ad.

If something is a dog, you either *fix it* (re-write the ads, reconfigure the Ad Group / bid / landing page) or you *kill it*. You don't just let it run and run, losing you money.

In summary, you're using these metrics to verify:

- Your ads are running vis-à-vis your target keywords by spot checking with the preview tool.
- Your SIS is > 85% meaning your ads are running most of the time.
- Your Position is < 5, meaning you're in the #1, #2, #3, or #4 positions, at the top of the Google page.
- Your CTR is > 1% or better.

AND

- Your CPC is as low as possible by reducing your bid yet retaining the metrics above.

The Bid Simulator: A Useless and Misleading Tool

Note: at the Ad Group level in the Default Max CPC column (indicating your bid), you can click on the little zig-zag arrow to enable Google's **Bid Simulator**. This attempts to tell you if you increased your bid, what will happen to your clicks, cost, and impressions. In my humble opinion, the Bid Simulator is a completely misleading tool. I have found that often if you *reduce* your bid, your clicks stay the same or even increase as Google seems to "work harder" to spend "all your money" at the lower click bid (despite what bid simulator will tell you). <u>I find more success systematically lowering my bids over time, yet paying attention to my SIS score and spot-checking my ads until I find the hidden "minimum bid" that Google wants to keep my ad running full blast.</u>

Don't believe everything Google tells you.

Tuning Your Ads to Hit the Trifecta

Let me repeat this, as it's important. Once you are running, *lower* the bids in any given Ad Group until your SIS falls below 85%, and then *raise* them back up. You want to tweak your bids down, paying attention to your SIS, and you may find that by lowering your bids you actually get more impressions and more clicks – the complete reverse of what the official Google help files tell you. So on a weekly or monthly basis:

1. Log in to AdWords, and drill into your Ad Groups.
2. If an Ad Group has a good CTR (> 1 or 2%) and a good SIS (> 85%), then lower your bid just a tad (perhaps by fifty cents or so – it depends).

If an Ad Group has a poor CTR, then you need to re-write or improve the ads. If an Ad Group has a good CTR but a poor SIS, then you need to increase your bids. What you are doing is "tuning" your bids and ads to try to hit the *trifecta* of a good CTR, a good position, and a good SIS score at the lowest bid possible. Don't trust Google to optimize your bids for you, paying just .01 more than the advertiser below you as that is not true in my humble opinion.

Quality Score: Another Misleading Metric

Similarly, while there is a **Quality Score** metric available in AdWords, it is also not reliable. To find it, you have to go to *Ad Groups > Keywords*, next click on *Columns > Modify Columns*. Find and enable Quality Score under *Attributes*. Here's a screenshot:

Attributes

☑ Quality Score   ☐ Est. first position bid

☐ Est. top of page bid   ☐ Est. first page bid

☐ Match type   ☐ Tracking template

☐ Final URL   ☐ Campaign type

That will enable it, so you can see it in your AdWords Reporting. Once you're enable it, you'll see a column called *Qual. Score*. Generally speaking, you want a Quality Score of 4 or higher, except remember that Google gets paid "by the click" and you make money "by the conversion," so you can have a high Quality Score for a keyword that is a dog (*doesn't convert and/or doesn't make you money*). Conversely, you can have a low Quality Score for a star (*converts well, makes you a lot of money*) for a high value keyword, and/or a keyword for which you have written a strong attract / repel ad.

You may even get a (misleading) message from Google that says "Rarely shown to low quality score" but your ad will actually still be running per SIS and/or spot checking!

So take Quality Score with a huge grain of salt! I am more interested in a) is my ad running (SIS), b) is it in a good position (top of the page), and c) is it converting on my website?

Who cares about Quality Score if a, b, and c are all working?

▶ MONITOR THE DISPLAY NETWORK AND/OR YOUTUBE

If you're running on the Display Network or YouTube, some of the above-mentioned metrics don't apply. SIS (Search Impression Share), for example, isn't available, and there's no easy way to spot check to verify your ads are actually running. You have to rely on impressions and click data as reported by AdWords directly. Position is also a bit misleading as on many sites in the GDN there is only one position, or perhaps two, and they don't easily line up as they do on Google. Most importantly on the GDN, you want to check (at least monthly if not more often), your **placements**.

Spot Check Your Placements

To do so, click into a Display Network Campaign > Ad Group, because placements "live" at the Ad Group level. Then click on *Placements* on the left. Then *Where Ads Showed* at the top. Sort by cost, and look for Placements that have lots of clicks, high costs, and/or few conversions. You're looking for "winners" or "dogs," meaning either placements that are performing well (high ROI as measured by a low CPC, high CTR, and good conversion rate) or performing poorly. If a placement is a "dog," then you probably want to block that placement by adding it to a negative placement list. I often look for outliers – placements that have a high spend and/or a high CPC, and few conversions.

> Your very important **TODO** on the Display Network is to look for "dog" or "nefarious" websites and block them immediately.

You can use the Filter tab to create a filter to check for "stars" and "dogs." For example, here's a screenshot for a Display Network filter called "Conversion Stars" meaning high ROI:

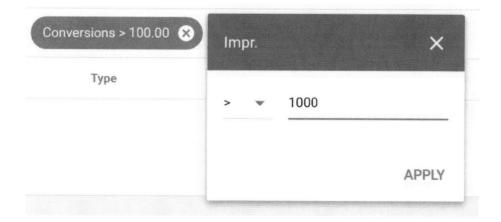

You can also create a filter for high impressions or cost, and low conversions to identify your "dogs." In this way, you can identify "winners" and "dogs," and continually improve your Google Display Network performance via placements.

YouTube

Remember that YouTube, parallel to the Google Search and Google Display Networks, has both a *Search* and a *Browse* functionality. Accordingly, if you are running YouTube ads using keyword targeting, click into an Ad Group, and then click *Keywords* on the left to view the keyword search queries on YouTube that generated impressions and views of your video. Here's a screenshot:

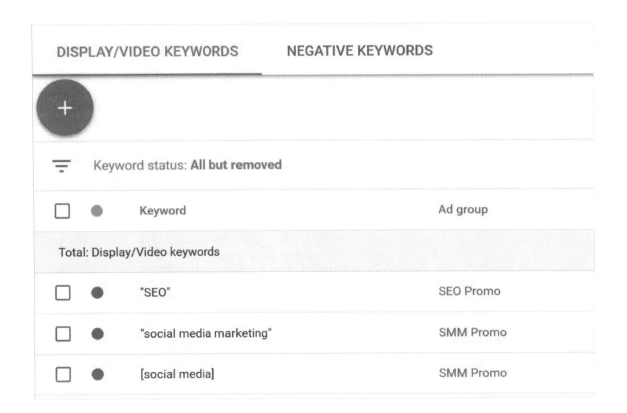

YouTube will also report clicks from the video to your call-to-action overlay, if enabled. If you're running on YouTube for browse (meaning "In-stream ads" or "Bumper ads"), you can click to the Placements tab and then see where your ads were run, either on YouTube or on the broader Google Display Network. To get even more detail, log in to your YouTube account and drill down to videos in Video Manager.

Using a Segment in Google Analytics for YouTube

Finally, inside of Google Analytics, you can set up a **Segment** to see, in more detail, how traffic from video ads on YouTube ended up on your website and whether it converted, as that data isn't easily available in AdWords or in YouTube itself. To set up this Segment, log into Google Analytics, click on the Grayed Out *+Add Segment* tab, then the red *+New Segment* button, then *Traffic Sources* and enter *youtube.com*. Here's a screenshot:

For the Google help file on how to create a Segment in Google Analytics, visit **http://jmlinks.com/25s**.

In summary, on both YouTube and the Google Display Network, you're looking to minimize your Cost Per Click (Cost Per View on YouTube), place your ads on the most relevant placements, secure the highest conversion rates and minimize total costs over time. I also strongly recommend that you continually monitor both the GDN and YouTube for "bad" or "nefarious" placements that just suck money out of your account.

» SET UP GOALS IN GOOGLE ANALYTICS

The Holy Grail for an advertiser on AdWords is a conversion. When you first conceptualize your AdWords strategy, you should identify what will constitute a conversion for you, such as:

These are "hard" goals –

A purchase on your e-Commerce store.

A completed inquiry form such as a sales inquiry.

These are "intermediate" goals –

A completed signup form such as an eLetter sign-up, free ebook or software download, etc.

A social media action such as "liking" your company's Facebook or LinkedIn page.

And these are soft goals –

Page views or time on site.

A video view

In most cases, the goal in Google Analytics can be measured as the *Thank You* page that the user hits AFTER they have completed the desired action. For example, after they fill out your inquiry form and hit send, they get to a *Thank You* page. Or, after they've made a purchase on your e-Commerce store, they get a *Thank You* for your order page.

Once you've defined these goals, I highly recommend that you log into Google Analytics, and define them as a "goal" in Google Analytics. To do this, go to the view page for your Website in Google Analytics, and find the ADMIN tab on the far left column. Click here, and then on the far right you should see Goals. Here's a screenshot:

VIDEO. Watch a video on how to set up goals in Google Analytics at **http://jmlinks.com/17z**.

Once a goal is set up, you can go back to the main page in Google Analytics, and use **Segments** to slice and dice your data and thereby see what traffic is converting (i.e., completing your goal) vs. what is not. (For help with goals, visit the official explanation at **http://jmlinks.com/19a**).

» SET UP CONVERSION TRACKING IN ADWORDS OR GOOGLE ANALYTICS

AdWords provides two ways to track conversions. Remember that a "conversion" is simply the successful completion of your "goal" such as a completed purchase on your e-Commerce store or a completed feedback form on your website. Once you've defined these as goals on your website, you have two methods to track them.

Method #1: AdWords Conversion Tracking

In AdWords, click on *Tools > Conversions*. Then click *Tools > Conversions*. Next, select the conversion type. Here's a screenshot:

For most of us, it will be "Website." Fill out the elements as indicated:

> **Name**. Give it a name such as "Contact Form"
>
> **Category**. Assign it a category as indicated.
>
> **Value**. Estimate its monetary value to your business.
>
> **Count**. Count every conversion.
>
> **Conversion Window**. Set it at the default of thirty days.

The default settings are generally fine. If you want to learn more, click on the "pencil icon" and then the "Learn more" link in blue. After you complete this, Google will give you some code to place on your website's *Thank You* page. Either copy/paste this yourself onto the "Thank You" page or have your developer install it. You can also use Google Tag Manager (**http://jmlinks.com/25u**) to manage this AdWords tag. You can verify your installation is correct using Google Tag Assistant (**http://jmlinks.com/25v**).

> **VIDEO.** Watch two good videos from Google on how to set up conversion tracking in AdWords at **http://jmlinks.com/41p** and **http://jmlinks.com/41q**.

Once you've successfully installed the AdWords Conversion tracking code, you should start to see conversions populating in your AdWords reports.

Method #2: Google Analytics

The second method is to use Google Analytics. I'll assume you've signed up for a Google Analytics account, and implemented the tracking code across your website. I'll also assume that you've set up goals in Google Analytics as indicated above. In general, it's better to use Google Analytics for your tracking system rather than just the AdWords code as it is more robust. You can get a lot more data in Google Analytics than in AdWords!

Next, you'll need to link your Google Analytics to your AdWords account.

Add Your AdWords Login Email

If you use the same login for both accounts, this is pretty easy. I'd recommend, at a minimum, that you make sure that the AdWords login you use is also listed as an Admin on Google Analytics. To do this (necessary only if your AdWords login is not the same as your Google Analytics login email):

1. Log in to Google Analytics.
2. Click on the Admin tab / far lower left column.
3. Click on "User Management" at either the account, property, and/or view level.
4. Add your AdWords login email to the list of users, and make sure it's added as a "Manage users, Edit, Collaborate, Read & Analyze" level account.

Here's a screenshot:

Link AdWords to Google Analytics

Next, you'll need to link your AdWords account to your Google Analytics account. Login to AdWords, and then click the Gear icon on the top right of the page. Then click "Linked accounts," and then click Google Analytics on the left column. You should see your Google Analytics account and then click the "Set up link" icon.

This can be a little tricky, so don't hesitate to call AdWords technical support by clicking on the Gear icon, and then finding the phone number. It's 866-246-6453 in the United States. The AdWords tech support team can walk you through how to link your AdWords to your Google Analytics account.

> **VIDEO.** Watch a video from Google on how to link Google Analytics to your AdWords account at **http://jmlinks.com/26s**.

Finally, once you've linked the two accounts, you should start to see conversions populating into your AdWords report. You should also **verify** that your account is linked by looking inside Google Analytics as follows:

1. Log in to Google Analytics.
2. Click on *Acquisition* on the left column.
3. Click on *AdWords*.
4. Click on *Campaigns*. You should see your AdWords Campaigns here.
5. Click on *Keywords* and *Search Queries*, and you should see those here.
6. **Important**: you should see Sessions data and Pages / Session data. This means that you can track behavior after the first page to see where people go on your website.

Finally, it's a good idea to create a Segment that is for just your AdWords traffic. To do this, click on the grayed out *+Add Segment* link at the top of the page in Google Analytics. (It's a little hard to see, so you may have to hunt for it). Here's a screenshot:

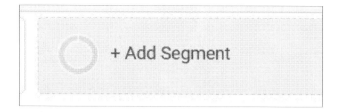

Next, click on *System* in the left column, and then find the Segment called *Paid Traffic* (if you are only advertising on AdWords). If you are advertising on other venues like Bing, Yahoo, or Facebook, click the red *+New Segment* button, give it a name like AdWords, then click *Traffic Sources* on the left, then *Medium* contains **cpc**, and *Source* contains **google.** Here's a screenshot:

| AdWords | Save | Cancel | Preview |

Traffic Sources
Segment your users by how they found you.

Demographics

Technology

Behavior

Date of First Session

Traffic Sources 2

Filter Sessions | Filter Users

Advanced

Conditions

Sequences

Campaign ? | contains ▾ |

Medium ? | contains ▾ | cpc

Source ? | contains ▾ | google

Keyword ? | contains ▾ |

At this point, you've set up goals in Google Analytics, correctly linked Google Analytics to AdWords, and set up a segment that allows you to examine the behavior of your AdWords-originating traffic exclusively. Be proud!

» REVIEW YOUR CONVERSION DATA IN ADWORDS

Now, let's return to AdWords and view the data inside of AdWords. Once you've activated goals and conversions in AdWords and/or Google Analytics, you should start to see conversions show up in your AdWords Reporting. If you remember that AdWords is a hierarchy, you'll be able to keep oriented as you view the following:

Conversions vs. Campaigns. *Which Campaigns are performing the best?*

Conversions vs. Ad Groups. *Which Ad Groups are performing the best?*

Conversions vs. Keywords. *Which Keywords are your best performers?*

Conversions vs. Ads. *Which ads are your top performers?*

You may not see Conversions showing up in the AdWords columns, so I recommend that at each level, you enable conversion data. At the Campaign level, for example, click on the *Columns icon*, then *Modify Columns*, and then click into *Conversions*. I recommend you enable:

Conversions. This will tell you the quantity of conversions. *More is better*.

Cost / conv. This will tell you how much you are paying to get a conversion. *Lower is better*.

Conv. rate. This will tell you the number of conversions / clicks. So, if you have 10 conversions out of 100 clicks, you have a 10/100 = 10% conversion rate. *Higher is better*.

If you've assigned a value to a conversion, or enabled e-Commerce tracking in Google Analytics, you can also enable value metrics in AdWords. These tell you not only the raw quantity of conversions but the value to you of a conversion as well. You can browse this data at the Campaign, Ad Group, Keyword, and Ad levels. You can also use the *Filter* tab to create a filter. For example, you can create a Filter to find Keywords for which you've spent more than $50 and the Cost per Conversion is > $10.

In this way, at any level (Campaign, Ad Group, Keyword, Ad) you can use a Filter in combination with Conversion data to identify "dogs" or "winners" and act accordingly.

If you've enabled the value metrics, you can use your conversion data to find out:

Quantity. Which Campaigns / Ad Groups / Keywords / Ads are generating the highest volume of conversions?

ROAS / ROI / Quality. Which Campaigns / Ad Groups / Keywords / Ads are generating the best *return on ad spend*, namely –

- o **Highest gross value**. Greatest dollar value as measured in sales volume.
- o **Most attractive performance**. Highest conversion rate, and highest revenue per conversion.
- o **Highest ROI**. Highest revenue per click as measured by highest value per conversion vs. click.

Time Horizons for Conversions

A Conversion in AdWords / Google Analytics defaults to a thirty-day window, so remember that if you are looking at very fresh data (e.g., *yesterday, last week*), you will tend to underestimate your conversions and overestimate your cost per conversion. In addition, the tracking isn't perfect, so AdWords / Google Analytics may significantly undercount conversions, not to mention fail to take into account lifetime customer value (LCV).

Use your gut instinct in combination with conversion data to verify that your AdWords advertising is working.

Conversions in Google Analytics

Google Analytics will give you even more robust data on conversions than AdWords. If you're using e-Commerce, for example, and you've linked your e-Commerce account to Google Analytics, Analytics will automatically populate e-Commerce sales as conversions and track the sales value. And, if Google Analytics is correctly linked to AdWords, then this **conversion value** will be populated in AdWords as well, automatically.

In this way, you can see the revenue per conversion data in Google Analytics as well as the raw conversion numbers.

You can also drill down into a Campaign, Ad Group, and/or Keyword to see which ones are generating the most clicks into your website and if the user fails to convert, you can follow the path from landing to bounce or exit. In this way, you can attempt to "debug" problems, wherein you are getting clicks from AdWords but not conversions. You can even use Analytics' Funnel Visualization tool to graphically represent the path from landing to conversion (or bounce / exit). Inside of Google Analytics, therefore, you have an even more detailed window into not only who clicks on your ads on AdWords, but what happens after the click, including those who convert easily at a high value and those who fail to convert or convert only at a low value.

>> IDENTIFY PROBLEMS AND OPPORTUNITIES

I recommend that, at first, you check your AdWords performance at least once a week. When you first start a new Campaign, I would even check it daily to make sure that it's actually running and that your spend and results are commensurate with your goals. Once you're up and running, then I find that – for most small business advertisers – checking twice a month is sufficient. (Obviously, if you are a large company or spending a significant amount, you'll want to check it more frequently).

Here's a list of things to check and opportunities to build out from; for each, at the *Campaign > Ad Group > Keywords > Ad level*. For our hypothetical Jason's Cat Emporium business, for example, we'd have at least two Campaigns (one selling cat accessories and one selling cat boarding & grooming). We'd then check each Campaign, as well as the Ad Groups inside them (both on the Search and on the Display Networks), especially with an eye towards keywords and conversions.

A Twice Monthly Checklist

At least once a week (at the beginning) and then twice-monthly, here are things to check at every level (Campaign / Ad Group / Keyword / Ad):

1. **Are your ads running?** Do a spot check using the Google AdWords *Ad Preview and Diagnosis* tool (on the Tools tab) to verify that your ads are actually running vis-à-vis your target keywords. If you're geotargeting, be sure to spot check various target cities. Check your recent performance to make sure you see impressions and clicks and check your **SIS score**.
2. **Double-check your Keywords.** What keywords are you running on as indicated by the "Search Terms" on the Keyword tab? Look for strong, valuable

keywords vs. bad matches or low-converting keywords. If keywords are erroneous or poor performers, consider blocking them as "negative keywords."

3. **What are your Impressions, Clicks, Average CPC, CTR, and Costs?** Do they look to be in the ballpark of what you want?

4. **What's Your Budget / Spend Month-to-date?** Check your budget at the Account, Campaign, Ad Group, and Keyword level to make sure it's within your budget. If it's too high, pause or bid lower on less lucrative keywords. If it's still too high, consider re-optimizing. It's better to run "full blast" on your high ROI keywords and not at all on low performers than to spread yourself too thin.

5. Do you see any **messages from Google** such as "Limited by Budget," "Below first page bid," or "Rarely shown due to low quality score?" If so, investigate and fix.

6. **Is your SIS > 85%?** How does that compare with your **Average Position** (< 4)? And what about your **CTR** (ideally, > 1%)? Adjust bids and/or re-write ads to attempt to hit the "happy medium" of SIS > 85% / average position of at least 4 / CTR > 1%.

7. **How are your conversions**? Which Campaigns and Ad Groups have decent conversion quantities, conversion rates, and conversion values? Which ones are high ROAS, and which ones are low?
   a. Look at the Keyword level at your conversions. Which keywords have decent or better conversions, and which are below average? Investigate and fix as needed.

8. As for the **Google Display Network**, be sure to check your placements (looking for nefarious or "dog" placements) as well as check your CTR's and conversion rates and values.

In addition to the above, be on the look out for "dogs" and for "winners." As for "dogs" – Campaigns, Ad Groups, Keywords, and/or Ads that are low performers – try to fix them as needed, and if necessary "kill" them. There's no shame in giving up on either non-winnable keyword patterns at an affordable price, or in realizing that some keywords are just "dogs." I will say it again:

KILL YOUR DOGS & LET YOUR WINNERS RUN

Pull Winners Out into their Own Special Ad Groups

As for "winners" or "opportunities," identify your best-performing Campaigns, Ad Groups, Keywords, and/or Ads and let them run. In particular, if you find keywords at the keyword level that are strong-performers, think of breaking them out into a special ad group.

> *Remember that Google rewards a tight linkage between your Ad Groups and Keywords, so if there's a high performing keyword, breaking it out into a specialized Ad Group will generally boost its SIS, position, click thru rate and even conversion rate.*

If for example, we learn that the phrase "luxury cat boarding" generated a high return on ad spend, then we'd break it out into a special Ad Group with special, unique ads just for it as well as a uniquely optimized landing page.

Situate AdWords ROI within Other Online Opportunities

Finally, don't forget to compare your return on investment through AdWords with your ROI from other Internet marketing methods, such as SEO and/or Social Media. In particular, use a tool like FatRank for Chrome (**http://jmlinks.com/25w**) and/or the AdWords Preview tool by city to see if you're ranking for "free" on Google with organic results. If you are ranking in the top three positions organically, then consider either cutting back on your AdWords spend for that keyword, redeploy those funds to other more needy keywords, or just be happy that you're crushing it with visibility via AdWords *and* via Organic for high-value keyword patterns.

If you're running on the Display Network or YouTube, consider trying out **social media advertising** on Facebook, Twitter, Instagram, or LinkedIn, as often performance on those social media networks will outperform that of the Google Display Network with its plethora of nefarious site partners. The ROI on **email marketing**, in particular, is one people often miss. So don't overspend on AdWords yet starve your email marketing efforts.

▶▶ DELIVERABLE: AN ADWORDS METRIC WORKSHEET

The **DELIVERABLE** for this chapter is a completed worksheet on AdWords Metrics.

For the **worksheet**, go to **https://www.jm-seo.org/workbooks** (click on "AdWords Workbook 2018," enter the code 'adwords18' to register if you have not already done so), and click on the link to the "AdWords Metric Worksheet."

8
AdWords Toolbook

AdWords is easier with tools. To that end, I've compiled a companion *AdWords Toolbook*. Register your copy of the AdWords Workbook, and you'll get full access to a PDF of all my favorite AdWords tools plus my handy "dashboard" with easy, clickable links. In addition, here are the *best of the best* – my favorite AdWords tools, ranked with the best ones first. To access the AdWords Toolbook for the complete list, go to **https://www.jm-seo.org/workbooks** (click on "AdWords Workbook 2018," enter the code 'adwords18' to register if you have not already done so), and click on the link to the *AdWords Toolbook*.

That said, here are my top tools for AdWords.

ADWORDS ACADEMY OF ADS - https://landing.google.com/academyforads/

Google's official training site for AdWords. Yes, a bit salesy and take it all with a huge grain of Google salt, but very good information by Google for Google about Google. #BeSkeptical.

Rating: 5 Stars | **Category:** resource

GOOGLE ACADEMY FOR ADS - https://academy.exceedlms.com/

Yet another view of the Google Academy for Ads. Google has 'outsourced' this to a third-party, but this is the official learning resource for AdWords.

Rating: 5 Stars | **Category:** resource

GOOGLE ADWORDS HELP CENTER - http://support.google.com/adwords

Your gateway to easy-to-use lessons about the Google AdWords advertising program. Whether you're just getting started with AdWords, seeking to improve your ad performance, or studying for the Google Advertising Professionals exam, you'll find lessons designed to help you learn at your own pace. You can also read the complete version (with all available lessons).

Rating: 5 Stars | **Category:** resource

GOOGLE INSIDE ADWORDS BLOG - https://adwords.googleblog.com/

The official blog for Google AdWords. It's more for sophisticated users than for newbies, but - that said - you should pay attention to it if you are spending money with Google.

Rating: 4 Stars | **Category:** blog

SEED KEYWORDS - http://www.seedkeywords.com/

This is a wonderful human / machine tool. Gather your team together (or they can be in diverse cities). Create a prompt, such as 'your hungry and you love Italian food, what would you search for?' This then creates a 'workspace' and as people type in their ideas it consolidiates them into a master list. Excellent and fun tool for keyword brainstorming!

Rating: 5 Stars | **Category:** tool

SERPS.COM KEYWORD TOOL - https://serps.com/tools/keyword-research/

Bye bye keyword planner and hello Keyword Tool. SERPS.com has done a great job on this easy-to-use, powerful, and FREE alternative to Google's Keyword Planner.

Rating: 5 Stars | **Category:** tool

SEOCHAT KEYWORD TOOL - http://tools.seochat.com/tools/suggest-tool/

This most awesome keyword suggest tool is like Ubersuggest, but pulls keyword suggestions not just from Google or Bing, but from YouTube, Amazon, etc. Awesome for keyword brainstorming.

Rating: 5 Stars | **Category:** tool

ADWORDS EDITOR - https://adwords.google.com/home/tools/adwords-editor/

AdWords Editor is a free, downloadable (Windows or Mac) application for managing large Google AdWords accounts efficiently. Download campaigns, make changes with powerful editing tools, then upload the changes to AdWords.

Rating: 4 Stars | **Category:** tool

GOOGLE ADWORDS KEYWORD PLANNER -
https://adwords.google.com/ko/KeywordPlanner/Standalone/Home

Who got the data? Google got the data. Use the Keyword Planner for keyword discovery for both SEO and AdWords, but be sure to know how to use it. Not the easiest user interface, and remember it ONLY gives data for EXACT match types. NOTE: you MUST have a paid account to use, and be LOGGED IN.

Rating: 4 Stars | **Category:** tool

ADWORDS YOUTUBE CHANNEL - https://www.youtube.com/user/learnwithgoogle

Official Google AdWords channel. Learn from the horse's mouth how to advertise on AdWords, why advertise, etc. Of course, be a bit skeptical as it is by Google, about Google, and ultimately for Google!

Rating: 4 Stars | **Category:** resource

SEM RUSH - https://www.semrush.com/

Similar to KeywordSpy, this tool allows you to enter a domain or a competitor, and returns a list of AdWords keywords they are running under as well as their organic keywords. Use it to track a competitor, as well as to generate a keyword list (keyword discovery).

Rating: 4 Stars | **Category:** tool

GOOGLE PARTNERS HELP CENTER - https://support.google.com/partners

Google partners is Google's platform for agencies and consultants, particularly for AdWords. However, you can 'join' as an individual and thereby get access to many wonderful FREE Google AdWords learning resources. If you are a serious learner with respect to AdWords, this is a great way to go behind the scenes and learn even more about AdWords.

Rating: 4 Stars | **Category:** resource

KEYWORD FINDER - https://kwfinder.com/

A very fun, interesting tool to discover keywords. Input some keywords, and get quick ideas for related terms, helper words, and more.

Rating: 4 Stars | **Category:** tool

TAG ASSISTANT FOR CHROME - http://tinyurl.com/tagasst

If you're using AdWords and Google Analytics to track conversions, you need to verify you have the right 'tags' running as Javascript on your website. Ask your developer to get the conversion tracking code from AdWords and install on ALL pages of your website. Then use this Chrome extension to double check / verify it actually is there.

Rating: 4 Stars | **Category:** tool

LOCAL RANK CHECKING VIA ADWORDS - https://adwords.google.com/anon/AdPreview

This is the OFFICIAL Google AdWords preview tool. But, guess what. You can use this to vary your city location, and check your rank against various cities. If, for example, you are a pizza restaurant serving San Jose, Milpitas, and Santa Clara, you can type in 'Pizza' and see your rank in different cities. You can login to your AdWord account and click Tools - Preview Tool or use this direct link.

Rating: 4 Stars | **Category:** tool

KEYWORDSPY - http://www.keywordspy.com/

KeywordSpy currently operates in USA, United Kingdom, Australia and Canada. Through this keyword tool and keyword software, you can perform advanced keyword research and keyword tracking to study what your competitors have been advertising in their AdWords campaigns and other PPC campaigns. You can get complete in-depth analysis, stats, budget, affiliates & ad copies of your competitors.

Rating: 4 Stars | **Category:** tool

MOAT AD SEARCH - https://moat.com/

Want to snoop on competitors? Steal their ad ideas? Enter Moat Ad Search. Enter a competitor name and Moat goes and finds all sorts of ads that they've posted across the Internet. Mainly the Display ads, but excellent to see how a company brainstormed its ad strategy.

Rating: 4 Stars | **Category:** tool

KEYWORD NICHE FINDER - http://wordstream.com/keyword-niche-finder

Really this tool is about finding related keywords. Enter a target keyword and the tool will generate a list of closely related keywords. Then click on any one of those, and the right hand side of the screen will show clusters of those related tools. It is a good tool for keyword discovery, not unlike Google's Wonder Wheel or related searches.

Rating: 4 Stars | **Category:** tool

GOOGLE ADWORDS COMMUNITY - https://en.adwords-community.com

This is the official Google AdWords community group, wherein users post questions and get answers from Googlers or other AdWords gurus on AdWords. It's a bit of a free-for-all but useful if you have a burning question about AdWords! Just remember that these are Google forums, so things can be on the salesy side.

Rating: 4 Stars | **Category:** resource

Made in the USA
Lexington, KY
30 September 2018